Alternatives to Abstinence

*A New Look at Alcoholism
and the Choices in Treatment*

Alternatives ^{TO}Abstinence

A New Look at Alcoholism and the Choices in Treatment

HEATHER OGILVIE

HATHERLEIGH PRESS
NEW YORK

Hatherleigh Press
An Affiliate of W.W. Norton & Company, Inc.
5-22 46th Avenue, Suite 200
Long Island City, NY 11101
1-800-528-2550

Printed in Canada

This edition is printed on acid-free paper that meets the
American National Standards Institute Z39-48 Standard.

Library of Congress Cataloging-in-Publication Data
To Follow

All Hatherleigh Press titles are available for bulk purchase,
special promotions, and premiums. For more information,
please contact the manager of our Special Sales Department
at 1-800-528-2550.

Designed by Anne Carpenter

10   9   8   7   6   5   4   3   2   1

For my father

Table of Contents

•

Foreword

IN MOST U.S. healthcare settings, the principle of informed consent is respected. The patient is fully informed about his or her diagnoses, treatment options and risks, and the level of confidence in the accuracy of each piece of information. Having reviewed the relevant information, the patient, in consultation with one or more healthcare providers, is free to choose a course of action.

In U.S. alcohol care (and other addiction services) the principle of informed consent and the steps necessary to implement it are less than routinely employed. In far too many instances providers do not adequately diagnose patients, inform them about the range of treatment options available, represent risks or areas of uncertainty accurately, or honor the patient's right to choose the course of action.

The failure of alcohol treatment providers to inform their patients adequately has had an impact on all of us. What most Americans believe about drinking problems and their treatment is substantially inaccurate. *Alternatives to Abstinence* contains the up-to-date, scientifically accurate information that our country (and in particular our alcohol treatment industry) needs in order to understand drinking problems and their treatment. It is ironic that the United States, which presumably leads the world in the quality of its healthcare, should in this one healthcare sector be so backwards. It is also tragic, because the United States has a greater need for addiction services than most other countries.

This book is the summary of what a clear-thinking, open-minded individual discovered after she spent months investigating the evidence about drinking problems and what is effective for overcoming them. Even if you desperately need the information covered in this book, very few individuals have the leisure to conduct the thorough investigation summarized here. With the help of this book, your education can be greatly simplified.

Drinking problems do not occur as a result of a disease process. Drinking is a learned behavior, which additional learning therefore can modify. Drinking is sometimes habitual, almost automatic. However, even in drinkers for whom it is highly habitual and acted on almost unconsciously, drinking behavior can be brought into full conscious awareness. Drinkers can then choose to drink or not to drink, to drink moderately or drink excessively. The choices they make will reflect, not a disease, but their understanding of what is truly important to them. Many individuals, even those with severe problems, are able to resolve drinking problems with little or no outside assistance. There are also various types of successful treatment approaches. No one approach works best for all individuals. Until we know more about matching treatments and drinkers, the best matching most likely occurs when the fully informed problem drinker chooses his or her own course of action, and persists until problems are resolved (or at least reduced).

If drinkers make choices about their drinking, they

will obviously also make choices about the kind of help they will access (to the extent they know about options for help). It is easily understandable that, in the early stages of making a drinking change, someone who is doing "too much of a good thing" will favor cutting back rather than stopping altogether. Typically, early change efforts are done privately. But even if outside help is sought, it seems likely that control of drinking rather than abstinence will be the initial goal. How unfortunate that this country's almost exclusive focus on abstinence probably keeps away individuals who would accept and benefit from an early moderation intervention. What if we treated all cases of high blood pressure only with medications and techniques aimed at severely high blood pressure? Those with borderline pressures would probably decide the cure was worse than the disease.

In my own treatment center, Practical Recovery Services, we stopped making a recommendation about moderation or abstinence years ago. We discovered that oftentimes our advice wasn't wanted, and that we didn't really know enough to predict who would be successful with either approach. Now we focus on helping our clients make a decision that fits their values, needs, and situations. This process can involve a lot of trial and error (and carries its own risks, which we also consider). Many clients learn to moderate their drinking. Many others decide (often before they even attend our center) that it is simpler and more practical to abstain.

I advise people not to focus on the moderation vs. abstinence debate to the point that they fail to see the benefits of behavior-based therapy. The same techniques that can help you stop after one, two, or three drinks can also help you stop before the first one (and vice versa). If you have drinking problems it's time to deal with them. You have in this book the information you need to get started.

A. Thomas Horvath, Ph.D.
President, Practical Recovery Services
    (practicalrecovery.com)
President, SMART Recovery (smartrecovery.org)
Past President, Division on Addictions (Division 50) of the
    American Psychological Association (apa.org)
Author of *Sex, Drugs, Gambling and Chocolate: A Workbook
for Overcoming Addictions* (Impact, 1999)

•

Preface

PROBLEM DRINKERS IN the United States are faced with a daunting dilemma when they seek help. They can either accept the prevailing myth that abstinence is the *only* effective means to resolve a drinking problem, or they can be accused of being "in denial" and dismissed from (or coerced into) an abstinence-only treatment that may be neither desirable nor appropriate for them.

How have we come to this position, unique among developed nations of the world (elsewhere a variety of options are available to problem drinkers who seek help), that takes a complex set of human issues and insists that they be addressed by a single approach? For no other "disease" is our approach to treatment so monolithic and so resistant to decades of research showing that there are a number of effective ways of helping people resolve drinking problems, some of them so brief in duration as to be hardly more than a short conversation between physician and patient. For no other "disease" do so many physicians, psychologists, social workers, and counselors, themselves, subscribe to the nonresearch-based myths that surround problem drinking, ignoring the research of their own colleagues in crafting their treatment approaches.

There are two central reasons why we treat problem drinking differently than other "diseases."

The first reason we adhere to abstinence as the *only* means of resolving problem drinking is that we have confused the *means* of resolving a drinking problem with the *goal* of doing so. Abstinence and moderation are but two *means* of achieving the real goal that every problem drinker attempting to change is seeking: a healthier, more contented life, free from alcohol-related problems. The goal of treatment is not only changing drinking patterns; the goal is also achieving more general lifestyle improvements that bring the individual's life into greater balance and harmony.

The second, more complex, reason has to do with the dominance in the United States of what I call the "cult of abstinence-only" for problem drinkers. This belief that abstinence is the only means for resolving drinking problems is deeply rooted in our heritage of religious fundamentalism. These roots grow deeply into the American psyche. They penetrate our society at all levels and are promulgated and promoted by the mass media, where pundits pontificate regularly about the need for adoption of a single treatment approach (typically one based on the twelve-step philosophy developed by Bill Wilson, one of the founders of Alcoholics Anonymous, itself a program heavily indebted to fundamentalist religion for its basic tenets). These individuals often justify this approach by offering, in somewhat narcissistic fashion, their personal experiences of recovery as the universal touchstone for "what works" in resolving problems caused by drinking alcohol.

Eminent sociologist Robin Room has pointed out that the unwillingness to accept alternatives such as moderation training or medications to assist in resolving problem drinking is as much rooted in our religious notions of redemption and deliverance from sin as it is in any objective life experience — either personal or scientific. We value people who have acknowledged the sin of alcoholism and have risen above it by renouncing forever the source of that sin: Demon Rum! To be a "recovering alcoholic" is to have a special status in our society — the status of one who has taken the Devil by the horns, battled, and emerged victorious.

Unfortunately, the "Devil" in question is not a uniform, monolithic one that is similar for all problem drinkers. Rather, drinking problems come in all shapes and sizes, and are as diverse as the people who experience them. Well-designed research conducted over more than three decades has conclusively demonstrated that the traditional view of problem drinking as being an inevitable harbinger of progression to the "disease" of alcoholism is simply wrong. Some problem drinkers "progress," but the vast majority don't. Likewise, research has shown that the core belief of the "cult of abstinence-only" — that the only way to fully resolve a problem with alcohol is to abstain for life — is also wrong for the vast majority of people who experience problems related to their drinking. Unfortunately, this research has been largely ignored by the media, whose portrayals of problem drinking continue to be simplistic, uninformed, and wrong. It is also ignored by many treatment professionals who, cowed by the threat of disapproval associated with publicly questioning the prevailing wisdom of the cult of abstinence-only, fail to take this solid work into account.

What does the research show us about the beliefs of the "cult of abstinence-only"? First, it shows that even when achieving abstinence is the primary focus of treatment, a substantial proportion of individuals becomes moderate drinkers. These individuals also show movement toward the goal of improved health — they no longer meet diagnostic criteria for an alcohol disorder, criteria based largely on the problems caused by alcohol in the person's life, despite the fact that they continue to drink in moderation. In a recent presentation, Dr. Patricia Owen, Director of Research of the Hazelden Foundation, long a bastion of abstinence-only treatment, referred to these individuals as "in recovery without abstinence" and acknowledged their presence in large numbers among a sample of Hazelden graduates. In fact, the proportions of abstinent and moderate drinkers following abstinence-focused treatment are about equal in study after study.

Second, the research shows quite clearly that when individuals themselves endorse and accept a means of resolving a drinking problem (whether it be abstinence or moderation), the chances of achieving resolution to the problem increase substantially. Finally, the research shows conclusively what clinical experience has shown for years — that no single approach works for every problem drinker. These three broad sets of findings suggest that what is needed is not continued insistence upon a single means of resolving problem drinking, but an increased diversity of means that can be offered to problem drinkers who seek to change.

There is a great need to bring the fruits of research on the resolution of problem drinking to the public. Thus, a book such as *Alternatives to Abstinence: A New Look at Alcoholism and the Choices in Treatment* is especially welcome. Drawing extensively on the best scientific research, Heather Ogilvie presents a readable, informative, and balanced overview of the current state of our knowledge about problem drinking and how problem drinkers might go about getting effective help. This approach takes some courage in times such as ours, when professionals who attempt to speak out about the research and implement it in practice are at risk of losing their jobs for not adhering to the cult of abstinence-only. Ms. Ogilvie shows that courage. She also shows the courage to remain balanced in her approach.

Abstinence-focused approaches should not be abandoned. Rather, they need to be amplified and augmented with the variety of other approaches, including moderation training and medications, that research has demonstrated are effective in helping problem drinkers reach the goal of healthier lives. Abstinence is the single sure means, if effectively implemented, to a certain resolution of problems with alcohol. That is a fact, and problem drinkers know it. When offered a choice between abstinence and moderation, research has consistently shown that most problem drinkers seeking treatment will choose abstinence. Not all, however, make this choice, and insistence by treatment programs on abstinence as the only means of resolving a drinking problem has actually been shown to deter many problem drinkers from seeking treatment. Nor is everyone able to effectively implement the total lifelong abstinence that treatment programs tell patients is required if they are to be truly "in recovery" (and thus become recipients of the cultural benefits of those who have "overcome sin"). In our current system in the United States, those individuals who want to choose means other than abstinence to resolve their problems with alcohol are directly confronted with the dilemma presented at the beginning of this preface: either accept a means they are not committed to or that may not be most appropriate for them, or be stigmatized as being "non-compliant" with treatment or "in denial."

What is needed is a treatment system that reflects

the diversity of the problems it aims to treat, one that offers both abstinence-focused and moderation-focused approaches, tailoring treatment to the needs of the individual, rather than attempting to deliver a "one-size-fits-all" approach. We need a treatment system that offers procedures that have been shown, both by personal experience and by well-done scientific research, to be effective, and one that recognizes the problem drinker's basic autonomy and responsibility as a human being to make the critical decisions about his or her life that determine the direction it will take, empowering the individual to take those measures, valuing the willingness to embark on the journey to health as much as reaching the final destination. This is certainly how good general medicine is practiced in the twenty-first century. Should problem drinkers be offered anything less?

Frederick Rotgers, Psy.D.
Assistant Chief Psychologist
Smithers Alcoholism Treatment and Training Center
St. Luke's-Roosevelt Hospital Center, New York, NY and
Chairman of the Board of Directors, Moderation
Management Network, Inc.

•

Acknowledgments

———————————————————————————————

T HE TOPIC OF alcoholism often inspires such passionate debates that each side is completely intolerant of the others' views. When it comes to a problem that can lead to the premature death of the individual as well as to the suffering of the family and community, it is no surprise that people express not only strong medical and moral opinions, but intense political and pragmatic concerns as well.

In researching the many books, articles, and scientific studies on this topic, I found it was always helpful "to consider the source." Does the author have an agenda? What are the author's background, credentials, and perspective? In determining these factors, I hoped to be able to present an accurate account of the history of alcohol research, the best scientific evidence to date, and the most successful treatments available. I realize that my motives and opinions, too, will be scrutinized, so I offer here some personal information.

Until my publisher approached me about writing a book on alternative treatments for alcoholism, I had neither any special expertise in the subject nor any personal experience with alcohol problems. Much of the scientific information I uncovered was news to me, and I was unaware that such a fierce debate raged over the so-called "disease theory" of problem drinking. I have edited a number of health books (on topics ranging from depression and anxiety to non-alcohol-related liver disease). I am a writer; I am not a therapist, scientist, doctor, or recovering alcoholic. Many fine books have been written by the latter, however, and I hope that my references to them in the text will inspire readers to seek them out for further information on the topic.

Among those whose work I have relied on heavily are University of Washington Psychology Professor G. Alan Marlatt; University of Northumbria Professor of Alcohol and Drug Studies Nick Heather and Trinity College Dublin Professor of Psychology Ian Robertson; University of New Mexico Professors of Psychiatry and Psychology William R. Miller and Reid K. Hester; University of California School of Medicine Professor Marc A. Schuckit; Harvard Professor of Psychiatry George E. Vaillant; philosopher Herbert Fingarette; attorney and social psychologist Stanton Peele; and Loyola College History Professor Thomas R. Pegram.

In addition to these scholars, I'm grateful for the assistance of artist, songwriter, and musicologist Brian Dewan, for his help researching temperance songs and for his drawing of the Cogswell Temperance Fountain on p. 22; and for the Foreword and Preface written by alcohol treatment specialists Dr. A. Thomas Horvath and Dr. Frederick Rotgers, respectively.

Finally, while it is my opinion that the availability of more treatment options will ultimately serve more sufferers of alcohol-related problems than do traditional treatment centers and twelve-step programs alone, I do not believe that any one treatment works best in every case. Nor do I recommend that anyone who has successfully maintained sobriety through one program should take it upon himself or herself to change treatment goals without first seeking professional assistance.

Heather Ogilvie
January 2001

•

1 Another Round

*"I read about the evils of drinking
so I gave up reading."*
–Henny Youngman

MOST AMERICANS THINK of problem drinking as the disease of alcoholism. They believe the problem drinker is a sick person who requires treatment. The public is also under the impression that the primary evidence corroborating that a heavy drinker has the disease is his unwillingness to admit it (in other words, his "denial").

Furthermore, when most Americans think of treatment for drinking problems, two things come to mind: twenty-eight-day inpatient recovery programs (such as the Betty Ford Center) and the "outpatient," twelve-step program of Alcoholics Anonymous (AA).

There are, however, at least a dozen alternative approaches to treatment that have been proven at least as effective as AA and inpatient programs (most of which are also based on the twelve steps of AA). Why are Americans largely unaware of these alternatives? Why are these treatments unavailable to the majority of Americans? And how can a person with drinking problems go about finding treatment that is best suited to his or her particular needs?

To answer these questions, one has to understand the way our society views alcoholism. Chapter 2 looks at the history of drinking in the United States and how our culture has looked upon people who have drunk excessively. From the birth of the temperance movement to the rise and fall of Prohibition to the dubbing of alcoholism as a disease and subsequent scientific inquiries into the nature of problem drinking, our society has grappled with how best to treat those whose drinking leads to personal and societal harm. In the past, we've demonized them, punished them, ostracized them, legislated against them, medicated them — and only rarely have we sought to treat them compassionately and pragmatically.

The roots of our current beliefs about the causes and nature of alcoholism go back to the 1930s — and, surprisingly, conflict with subsequent scientific research. The so-called "disease theory" of alcoholism pervades popular beliefs about problem drinking and has sparked intense — at times vitriolic — debates among the twelve-step treatment industry and researchers in various branches of science. Chapter 3 examines the disease theory and the evidence supporting it; Chapter 4 considers the evidence against it; and Chapter 5 describes the concepts of problem drinking accepted by scientists, many physicians, and most treatment professionals outside the United States.

Certainly people could debate all day the definition of "disease," let alone the definition of "alcoholism." What does it matter what we call the problem? After a shift in semantics, would we treat the problem drinker any differently?

How we think about the nature of problem drinking turns out to have an important impact on how we, as a society, treat problem drinkers, fund treatment research, and make laws regarding alcohol abuse. And, perhaps most important, how a heavy drinker thinks about the nature of her problem — as a progressive disease, an inherited condition, a behavioral disorder, or a bad habit — may figure prominently in how well that person responds to treatment. Chapter 6 considers the pros and cons of thinking of problem drinking as a disease, whether or not it meets certain medical or scientific criteria.

Finally, Chapter 7 describes the treatment approaches that have proven to be at least as effective as twelve-step methods, which are also examined in detail.

Why Seek Alternatives?

It has been said that there are as many causes of alcoholism as there are alcoholics. Some people drink to ease anxiety; some drink to heighten their sense of excitement; some drink to enhance their feelings of power or overcome feelings of inferiority; some to overcome loneliness; some to fit into a group. Some people drink in social settings; some drink alone. Environmental, psychological, physiological, genetic — all these factors combine to create the problem drinker. With so many factors at play, it is hard to believe alcoholism could have any one cause.

Likewise, it may be naïve to think that there could be any one treatment. Recognizing the diversity among problem drinkers has led treatment professionals, researchers, policymakers, and insurers to admit that no one program can solve every individual's problem. Arming treatment professionals with an arsenal of approaches not only makes sense, but may introduce two aspects to treatment that could prove especially beneficial to the individual: choice and a sense of control. These two elements, however, are absent from conventional twelve-step programs, which are based on an understanding of alcoholism as a disease that, by their definition, causes a person's loss of control and impairs his abilities to make decisions in his own best interest.

Believing one has even a modicum of control of over one's fate, however, is proving important to the treatment of many illnesses. Take, for example, breast cancer. A woman diagnosed with this disease is likely to get a second opinion about the appropriate treatment, do research on her own about the disease and its treatments, and actively participate in her treatment by making changes in diet and exercise habits. By feeling as though she's supplementing her medical treatment, her mind-set is positive, rather than defeatist or passive. Indeed, many experts believe that mental outlook contributes in some measure to patients' recovery outcomes.

Not too long ago, a patient receiving a diagnosis of heart disease would rely solely on medicine — pills or surgery — to treat the problem. Heart disease was seen as beyond the patient's control. For several years now, however, doctors have been trying to get patients to understand their roles and responsibilities in treatment. Doctors recommend exercise and dietary changes, and delay more invasive treatments until they can evaluate the benefits of the changes in the patient's behavior.

Doctors, family members, friends, or employers who encourage a problem drinker to get help usually have only one treatment option to recommend: AA. The information this organization presents to the drinker is unequivocal. In twelve-step recovery programs, the client is told (a) his drinking is beyond his control — in fact, he is powerless against it, (b) his condition is irreversible and incurable, and (c) the success of the treatment depends solely on a Higher Power. While that Higher Power may be the god of any religion, the group, or another person, it must be a power *other than* the individual. A person who prefers to see *himself* as the effective power, therefore, would not find AA helpful in improving his sense of self-efficacy, his (supposedly absent) self-control, or his willpower not to take another drink.

What often happens when a diagnosed alcoholic in a twelve-step recovery program has a drink — just one — is that she sees herself as a total failure. She is then likely to think, Well, I've blown it, so I may as well as go all out. Success is an all-or-nothing, black-or-white matter. Falling off the wagon thus only proves to the drinker what she has been told: that she has no control. Henceforth, what is her motivation to keep attending AA or to seek further treatment? Furthermore, treatment professionals who advocate twelve-step programs would typically regard her relapse not as a failure of treatment, but as a failure of the patient to comply with her treatment. Given these conditions, it is no wonder so few people are able to maintain long-term sobriety through twelve-step recovery programs.

Other, non-disease-based concepts of problem drinking and their treatment models seek to give back to the patient a sense of control, responsibility, power, and hope. They seek to motivate the patient regardless of her spiritual beliefs and in spite of temporary relapses. They aim to draw problem drinkers into treatment sooner, before they hit "rock bottom" or require medical detoxification or treatment for alcohol-related diseases like cirrhosis.

AA in Perspective

Proponents of alternative treatments do not necessarily have a beef against Alcoholics Anonymous. Since its founding in the mid-1930s, the fellowship of AA has undoubtedly saved countless lives. The people who are able to maintain sobriety through AA should certainly continue to attend meetings. But AA does not work for everyone.

Various estimates suggest that more than half of the people who attend AA meetings drop out within the first year. Of the people who regularly attend meetings, only about 25 percent succeed in a goal of long-term abstinence. Most professionals performing alcohol-related research today aim to make available treatment options that can help the problem drinkers for whom AA does not work or does not appeal, as well as for those who never even try AA.

Unfortunately, few treatment options have better outcomes than AA: 25 percent is about the best any one program can boast. This is not great news, as it is estimated that a third of all problem drinkers cut down or quit drinking on their own. To even suggest that some problem drinkers recover on their own is heresy to the advocates of the disease model, as alcoholism is, by their definition, irreversible. They argue that those drinkers who appear to have reduced their drinking to moderate, non-problematic amounts were never true alcoholics to begin with. This thinking is not particularly helpful from a treatment perspective, however, as it makes it impossible to tell a "true" alcoholic from a mere heavy drinker until serious damage has been done. Matching drinkers to the appropriate treatment may yield better recovery outcomes, and studies have indicated that informing drinkers of their treatment options and the beliefs behind them may yield the best outcomes of all.

A limitation of AA and inpatient recovery programs is that they tend to attract only late-stage alcoholics — those who already experience severe withdrawal symptoms when they try to quit. Where would a heavy drinker who has not experienced severe problems but who wants to learn to cut back go for help? If this person's drinking is not affecting his job, his relationships, or his day-to-day health, he is not likely to consider himself an "alcoholic" or sick, which is the first step of AA's twelve-step program and a prerequisite of twenty-eight-day treatment center admittance. The treatment "system" as it exists in the United States usually fails to attract heavy drinkers and help prevent them from becoming problem drinkers.

The Struggle for Control

The most controversial alternative treatments are those that have reduced or moderate drinking as their goal, rather than abstinence. While it may seem a perfectly reasonable approach for a smoker to cut back before quitting, when it comes to alcoholism, the same strategy of gradually cutting back somehow seems too dangerous and too unethical to even recommend. This belief is so deeply ingrained in our thinking that when we want to describe something that is cruel or unproductive we often say it's like "giving a drink to an alcoholic."

For people who have experienced alcohol-related problems for more than twenty years, for those who have been hospitalized for the delirium tremens, and for those whose laboratory tests indicate liver or other

organ damage as a result of alcohol abuse, total abstinence is undoubtedly the most prudent goal. There is
considerable evidence, however, that those who are
younger than 40 and who have experienced less severe
drinking problems may be good candidates for programs aimed at moderate or so-called "controlled"
drinking. In fact, there is ample evidence that many formerly diagnosed alcoholics moderate their drinking
without any outside help at all. *No one would recommend, however, that currently abstinent alcoholics begin
drinking again on their own — the achievement of stable
sobriety is too valuable to risk.*

How does one distinguish between "normal" and
"problem" drinking? Problem drinking is alcohol consumption that leads to recurring incidents of violence,
legal trouble, hospital admittance, drunk driving
arrests and accidents, marital and family problems,
and employment problems. (The sidebar on page 16
provides further information.) As a country, we have a
lot of problem drinkers. Various sources put the figure
between 7 and 10 percent of the population, or up to 20
million Americans. Nearly 100,000 people die each year
from alcohol-related problems. Crime reports reveal
that in 37 percent of the rapes and sexual assaults
reported annually the offenders have used alcohol.
Nearly half of all traffic fatalities each year· involve
alcohol.

Furthermore, the National Institute on Alcohol Abuse
and Alcoholism (NIAAA) recently reported an annual
estimate of the total cost of alcohol abuse to be $184.6
billion, or roughly $683 for every man, woman, and
child in the United States.[1] Problem drinkers and their
families bore about 45 percent of the estimated total
cost, the government bore roughly 40 percent, and private insurance bore approximately 15 percent.

It is not surprising, therefore, that treatment professionals are quick to label as "alcoholic" anyone who has had any problems as a result of drinking, regardless of their severity. One might even say it's prudent. To take it to the extreme, however, the most prudent way to eliminate problems due to alcohol abuse would be to reenact Prohibition. The surest way to eliminate car accidents would be to eliminate cars. As such things are not likely to happen anytime soon, how we diagnose drinking problems and whom we choose to treat are important matters.

Are college "binge" drinkers alcoholics? Are, as some people claim, the children of alcoholics, who may have never even sipped a drink, alcoholics themselves by genetic predisposition? If we believe they are, is spending time and money trying to persuade them to avoid even the smallest drop of alcohol a good use of resources? Is saddling these people with the notion that they are "diseased" really helping them?

The people in our country who have the most problems with alcohol — who most often end up in emergency rooms, jails, and driving accidents as a result of excessive drinking — are 18- to 25-year-old males. These are predominantly college binge drinkers; they are not the people who spring to mind as typical alcoholics, nor do they comprise the majority of clients admitted to residential recovery programs, who are usually over 40.

Student binge drinkers show a certain amount of control over their alcohol consumption that the stereotypical alcoholic — the one who needs a "hair of the dog" first thing in the morning and the comfort of knowing a bottle is always nearby — does not. These students do not drink during the week when they have classes; instead, they drink excessively on Friday or

Saturday nights. Yet, in our country, there are few educational efforts directed at this demographic or programs designed to help binge drinkers reduce their drinking. It is no wonder that abstinent-only treatment programs turn off these young people, who would have to face being labeled "alcoholic" and abstaining for the rest of their lives.

If alcoholism is the progressive, irreversible disease the twelve-step treatment industry would have us believe, one would expect these young problem drinkers eventually to become the 40-year-old clients of inpatient recovery programs. But they typically don't. Studies that followed young male problem drinkers found that 80 percent "outgrew" their behavior (Chapter 4 discusses this further). Most of the men claimed it was a phase they went through and that their behavior changed as soon as they left college, started jobs, or got married — in other words, when they found themselves in environments that were not as tolerant of, or as conducive to, binge drinking. They most often accomplished this return to "normal" drinking without the intervention of AA or treatment programs. But during their "binge years," do young people have access to help aimed at reducing their risky behavior, help that understands their problems may be temporary? Typically, no. It appears as if the people in our country who have the greatest problems with alcohol, however short-lived, are the ones our treatment industry overlooks.

One of the benefits of controlled-drinking approaches is that people who would otherwise shun treatment, such as college-age drinkers, would seek the help of qualified professionals. But controlled drinking is certainly not for everyone.

As stated previously, while no one treatment

approach has been proven more effective than another in *all* cases, particular approaches seem more suited to individual cases. In fact, treatments, whether abstinence-oriented or with moderate drinking as the goal, seem to be most effective when the problem drinker actually helps to choose her treatment. To repeat, however, *no one is suggesting that a former problem drinker who is currently abstinent and attending AA should take it upon herself to experiment with "controlled drinking" without professional guidance.* Such a possibility, naturally, is the main objection the alcoholism treatment industry has to the publication of controlled-drinking treatments.

The debates among scientists, treatment professionals, doctors, lawyers, politicians, and even a noted philosopher have been impassioned, to say the least, and at times downright nasty. As one prominent disease-theory writer noted back in 1983:

> Scientists in the laboratory accuse the clinicians, who work directly with alcoholics, of ignoring scientific data and conforming to old-fashioned and outdated treatment methods. Clinicians accuse the scientists of dismissing all first-hand experiences with alcoholics as "nonscientific" and therefore invalid. Government administrators chide the scientists for their "intellectual arrogance," while the scientists accuse the bureaucrats of pandering to fads and special interests. Psychiatrists fret about being displaced from their positions as primary therapists and treatment personnel by a new wave of paraprofessionals specifically trained in alcoholism diagnosis and treatment.[2]

Despite the fact that controlled-drinking treatments have been around for thirty years and are accepted by both researchers here and treatment professionals abroad, traditionalists and the media continue to portray controlled drinking as though it were a new, radical, untested approach. It seems likely that strong opinions will continue to rage in the near future.

Science in Perspective

We Americans put a great deal of faith in science. We eagerly anticipate new drugs and new technology that will solve our problems and make life easier. It would seem unthinkable that our clinicians — the people who treat our problems — would rail against scientists, even vilify them, and thwart their research efforts.

Yet in the field of alcohol research and treatment that is exactly the case. Granted, each side has a lot at stake that has nothing to do with the person seeking treatment: The scientist seeks to have her research publicly accepted so that she may receive funds to continue her work and extend her livelihood. The clinician seeks to preserve a treatment approach so that he can keep charging clients — and their insurance providers — for his services. (A considerable bill it is: nearly $15,000 for the typical twenty-eight-day residential treatment program. That's close to $500 a day, of which private insurance may pay over half. This figure is comparable to the rates of hospitals and four-star hotels, sans round-the-clock professional medical supervision or room service.) Any scientific research that calls into question the effectiveness of such treatment will understandably meet industry resistance.

So, despite our great faith in science and technology,

it's not as though we don't ignore science when it suits us. Scientists tell us our industrial waste and vehicle emissions are damaging, if not destroying, our atmosphere, yet it does not seem an urgent enough problem for us to give up or rapidly change our manufacturing processes or driving habits. We may judge the benefits of such changes in economic, rather than in strictly scientific, terms. We may question whether some scientists are being too alarmist in order to get their names in the papers. It is our choice to ignore them.

But in the field of alcoholism, the general public has not had much of a choice. Clinicians in the treatment industry and twelve-step advocates, most of whom are not medical doctors, go out of their way to make sure that scientific discoveries regarding the nature and treatment of alcoholism do not make it into the mass media, and, when such reports appear, they launch expensive media campaigns against them.

One recent example involved the Smithers Addiction Treatment and Research Center in New York City. Along with the Betty Ford Center and the Hazelden Foundation, Smithers is one of the strongholds of the Minnesota Model of treatment, which is based on the twelve steps of AA and mandates total abstinence. In the July 10, 2000, issue of *New York* magazine, the head of addiction medicine for the hospital that oversees Smithers, Dr. Alex DeLuca, was quoted as saying, "We do find that people who go to twelve-step meetings do better, but it doesn't work for some, and I'm not going to tell them, 'Come back after you have suffered some more and are ready to do it our way.' I can't operate that way as a physician." He implied that Smithers was offering limited treatment with moderation, rather than abstinence, as the goal. His comments inflamed the passions of the president and board of the Smithers

Foundation, who promptly ran a full-page ad in *The New York Times* denouncing controlled-drinking treatment as an "abomination" and an "insult" to their founder's memory. Dr. DeLuca was forced to resign.

That someone should lose his job over a seemingly innocuous, pragmatic statement is reminiscent of the dismissal of former Surgeon General Jocelyn Elders in 1994. When confronted with the rise in pregnancies and sexually transmitted diseases among teenagers, she advocated more sex education in America's classrooms, an idea that rubbed some parents the wrong way. Certain religious groups objected to her proposal of teaching teens about condom use, lest they get the impression that their teachers were endorsing premarital sex. Elders did not back down; in fact, she elaborated, suggesting that perhaps masturbation should be discussed in schools as part of human sexuality, a possible alternative to abstinence for the relief of sexual urges. For this suggestion she was forced to resign. Realistically, the words "adolescence" and "masturbation" are practically synonymous, and one could argue that to think otherwise is extremely naive; but the public was not comfortable hearing such frank language at that time.

A great deal of publicity surrounded the June 2000 arrest of Audrey Kishline, the founder of the moderate-drinking support group Moderation Management for vehicular manslaughter as a result of drunk driving. (Kishline was actually a member of AA, not Moderation Management, at the time of her accident.) The board of Smithers and other traditionalists have proclaimed her accident as "proof" that moderate drinking programs don't work. It is worth pointing out, however, that countless alcoholics who have attended AA or other abstinence-oriented programs have also had relapses, no doubt with results equally as tragic and harmful to other people. Focusing on one celebrity's tragedy no more constitutes proof than does focusing on one celebrity's successful experience in a program: It does not indicate that one treatment is appropriate for all people. The issue is far more complex, as the following chapters attempt to illustrate. (For more information on the individual case of Audrey Kishline, see the Web site of attorney and moderation-advocate Stanton Peele at www.peele.net.)

The effort to discredit scientists whose findings conflict with popular beliefs may recall reactionary religious zeal opposed to, say, evolution or to the roundness of the earth. But science isn't always right, and it is not always appropriate. It has no place, for example, in matters of spirituality. In addition, scientific progress bumps up against ethics almost daily. Take, for example, genetic research. If we can manipulate human or cow or pig genes in order to create replacement organs for cancer patients, should we? If we can genetically manipulate embryos in the womb, should we? If aborted fetuses can be used to develop cures for cancer, should we allow scientists to use them in research, thus seeming to "endorse" abortion?

These are tough questions. But the point is that the general public is aware of them. People have the opportunity to see both sides and form their own opinions. In the area of alcoholism, an area that affects not only individual, but also public, health, and which many treatment professionals insist is a disease, science certainly should have a say. And the general public, not only treatment providers, should hear what it is.

This is not to say that all scientists agree on the nature of and best treatments for alcohol dependence and alcohol abuse. But making the scientific research and viewpoints more accessible is one of the aims of this book. The more informed we are about a problem, the better our decisions will be regarding its solutions.

•

"Normal" Drinking vs. "Problem" Drinking

Even the most severely dependent alcoholics do not drink continually, twenty-four hours a day, seven days a week. So when does a person go from being a normal drinker to being a problem drinker, or, in popular terminology, an alcoholic?

That is rather like asking when a person becomes old. There is no one age that defines the limit of youth; there is, so to speak, a gray area. A 40-year-old person may appear and act much older than a 50-year-old person, for example. The boundary separating young from old is highly subjective.

Another example is obesity. At what point does a person become overweight? Each individual has his own ideal weight range based on his height, age, bone structure, body mass index, etc. Does the scale alone tell him he is overweight, or do tests of cholesterol, blood pressure, and cardiovascular capacity contribute to a diagnosis? Furthermore, the weight that a doctor might consider within his patient's healthy range may be quite a bit higher than the patient's — or society's — aesthetic ideal.

Likewise, diagnosing alcoholism is not as simple as coming up with a single number that means the same in every person's case. Number of drinks consumed per day, for example, is not always an accurate indicator of a problem. It is possible that a 300-pound man may, without noticeable physical or social consequences, consume six shots of liquor a day, an amount that might render a 120-pound woman unconscious. Excessive drinking can certainly contribute to the development of liver disease, kidney disease, pancreatitis, ulcers, and other illnesses, but someone who develops cirrhosis as a result of excessive "binge" drinking may not necessarily exhibit signs of alcohol dependence. Societal norms also come into play. What the French consider normal daily wine consumption might challenge the average American's beliefs about moderation. Nevertheless, few people would accuse France of being a nation of alcoholics.

That said, general guidelines have nonetheless been proposed. One expert has defined binge drinking (constituting alcohol abuse but not alcohol dependence) as consuming more than four drinks on one occasion at least once in the past month and heavy drinking as consuming more than four drinks on five or more occasions in the past month. (One drink equals one shot of hard liquor, one glass of wine, or one bottle of beer.) Problem drinking would be consuming more than four drinks daily, as "multiple alcohol-related problems, physiological dependence, and problems with control are rare in men who do not exceed an average of four drinks a day."[3] Another expert has classified moderate drinking as fewer than thirteen drinks a week, or one to three drinks per day, and heavy drinking as anything more than that.[4] Guidelines for women are lower. For instance, the USDA defines moderate drinking as two drinks per day for men, one drink per day for women. In the following chapters, references to drinking that is "problem" and "heavy," as well as "moderate" and "normal" will be based on these general guidelines. Simply stated, "problem drinking" is alcohol consumption that causes repeated social, legal, physical, marital, or employment difficulties.

What are the most reliable warning signs that a person has a drinking problem? Dr. George Vaillant, author of *The Natural History of Alcoholism Revisited*, ranks the following symptoms of alcohol dependence:

- Admits problem with control
- Family/friends complain
- Morning drinking
- Problems with health
- Problems with job
- Blackouts
- Going on the wagon
- Diagnosis by clinician
- Marital problems
- Three-plus alcohol-related arrests

- Single hospital, clinic, or AA visit
- Financial problems
- Employer complaints[5]

Another measure of the adverse effects of alcohol is blood alcohol level (BAL), also known as blood alcohol concentration (BAC). A person's BAL is the amount of alcohol in the bloodstream, measured in milligrams of alcohol per 100 milliliters of blood. For example, a BAL of .10 means that alcohol represents one-tenth of 1 percent (or one one-thousandth) of one's total amount of blood.

Upon drinking, alcohol reaches the bloodstream fairly quickly. As soon as it enters a person's stomach, it is absorbed directly into the blood. The less food there is in the stomach, the more quickly alcohol will be absorbed.

The liver can process alcohol at the rate of roughly one drink per hour (approximately one ounce of 100-proof whiskey or three ounces of wine). The excess remains in the blood, affecting the BAL. The larger a person is, the more blood he will have, and the more he will have to drink to reach the same BAL as a smaller person.

When a non-alcohol-dependent person has one drink, her physical and mental functioning, including memory, concentration, attention span, and creative thinking, actually improve.[6] It's easy to see, then, why someone who has one drink would want to keep drinking. But when a person drinks more than an ounce of alcohol within an hour, these processes slowly become impaired. In other words, when it comes to alcohol, it doesn't take much to get too much of a good thing.

In addition to its psychotropic effects, alcohol packs another punch: an instant boost to one's blood sugar. One alcoholic drink can contain more sugar than a can of Coca-Cola. People who suffer from low blood sugar, also known as hypoglycemia, may find alcohol gives them immediate relief. Or, as Ogden Nash summed it up, "Candy/ Is dandy/ But liquor/ Is quicker." The peril of using alcohol to combat low blood sugar, however, is that the rise in blood sugar is short-lived and followed by a subsequent "crash" to low blood sugar levels.

In terms of blood alcohol level, after the first drink, which may indeed make the person temporarily sharper, the blood alcohol level may rise to .03. Beyond .05, the person's physical coordination is likely to become impaired. At .08, the drunk driving limit, both coordination and judgment are compromised. At .10, the person will clearly display intoxicated behavior in terms of mood, balance and coordination, and reaction time. A person will typically pass out with a BAL of .30, and death can occur with a BAL over .40.

•

2   A History of Drinking

FROM COLONIAL TIMES to Prohibition, Americans' attitudes toward alcohol have run the gamut. Alcohol has been seen as nutritious, medicinal, or poisonous. Drinkers have been considered socially responsible, morally weak, evil, or sick. Opinions about strong drink and hard drinkers have been constantly changing, right up to the present.

In the seventeenth and eighteenth centuries, colonists in the New World believed alcohol to be more healthy (and indeed probably safer) than water. Even Puritan preachers like Increase Mather extolled the benefits of drink from their pulpits. Politicians, including George Washington, plied voters with liquor during campaigns — an accepted practice. Men and women looked upon alcohol favorably, as a social lubricant and an aid to digestion and relaxation after a day of manual labor.

The people who drank to excess had few social problems as a result. Pre-industrial society offered few

Brian Dewan

The Cogswell Temperance Fountain in Washington, DC, quenched the thirsts of passersby during Prohibition. Sheltering the fountain's two coiled fishes, the heron-topped roof proclaims the cardinal virtues, one on each side of the fountain: FAITH, HOPE, CHARITY, and . . . TEMPERANCE. Although alcohol now flows freely in the country, the fountain has long since run dry.

dangers. Nearly everyone drank — men in the tavern, women at home — and the quantities they drank would seem to us today to be of "alcoholic" proportions. Drinking at the tavern was *the* social and entertainment activity, as central to colonial culture as watching television is to ours.

Shortly after the formation of the United States of America, alcohol seeped into political matters. As people began to envision how the new government could reform society according to democratic, Christian, and various other ideals, early temperance groups began to form. According to historian Thomas R. Pegram, author of *Battling Demon Rum,* these early reformers emphasized "self-control for the temperate and self-improvement for the troubled drinker."[1]

Indeed, American concepts of self-governance and self-reliance informed early opinions of alcohol use and abuse. Over the years, however, the temperance message shifted its emphasis from individual control toward government control by demanding legislative action to regulate, and eventually prohibit, alcohol sales and consumption.

Early Diagnosis

In 1785, prominent citizen Dr. Benjamin Rush proposed the first "disease concept" of chronic drinking in *An Inquiry into the Effects of Ardent Spirits upon the Human Body and Mind, With an Account of the Means of Preventing and of the Remedies for Curing Them.* A signer of the Declaration of Independence and a friend of Benjamin Franklin and Thomas Jefferson, Rush was wary of the addictive nature of hard liquor and recommended avoiding it entirely; however, he had no qualms about drinking beer or wine. He wrote from the perspective of promoting general public health, rather than of curing individuals. Proponents of temperance adopted Rush as their patron saint, overlooking his favorable views toward beer and wine. Hence, Rush became known as the father of the American temperance movement.

Shortly after the publication of Rush's *Inquiry*, another disease concept appeared in Edinburgh. In 1804, Dr. Thomas Trotter published an essay entitled *On Drunkenness*. He proposed that drunkenness was a "disease of the mind" that caused disorders of the body. Trotter recommended abstaining from all alcohol, including beer and wine, and "realized the futility of simply moralizing and preaching to the patient. He was aware of the importance of the environment and recognized that it was not good enough simply to return the patient to the same conditions he had come from."[2]

In England, however, this view of drunkenness as a disease did not sit well with the Church:

> By elevating "depravity" to the status of "disease" and insisting that the victim was not responsible for his actions, Trotter threatened society's moral code over which the Church stood guardian ... .
>
> By shifting the blame from the alcoholic's character to a "remote cause" outside the alcoholic's control, Trotter's new theory confused the lines between "good" (that is, willpower, self-control and moderation) and "evil" (that is, weakness of character, gluttony and intemperance).
>
> The medical profession was equally upset by Trotter's essay, which suggested that the

treatment of this "disease" was mainly their responsibility.[3]

It was not until 1849 that the terms "alcoholic" and "alcoholism" were coined by Swedish physician Magnus Huss. In nineteenth century America, however, the terms "inebriate" and "chronic inebriation" were the medical profession's terms of choice. Doctors had begun treating drinkers for chronic inebriation by 1841, when the first institution for inebriates opened in Boston. By 1900, more than fifty public and private facilities were dedicated to the treatment of inebriates.[4]

As chronic inebriation was seen as an addiction, a group of physicians and institution directors founded the Association for the Study of Inebriety in the 1870s. A short-lived quarterly publication, *The Journal of Inebriety*, encouraged research into alcohol-related issues.

Tipplers and Teetotalers

In the early 1800s, alcohol consumption rose to its highest per-capita levels in U.S. history. The average American citizen over age 14 drank more than twice as much as the average American adult today. The beverages of choice were beer, hard cider, and rye whiskey. Drunkenness was acceptable behavior at special occasions, including weddings, funerals, and holidays.

The increase in consumption was accompanied by an increase in public drunkenness and violence. Men stayed at taverns longer, neglecting their wives and children. These conditions drew women into the temperance movement. As a result, throughout the 1800s, women's issues, such as suffrage and improvement in education, were bound up with the politics of temperance.

The Massachusetts Society for the Suppression of Intemperance, established in 1813, was one of the first reform groups. The American Temperance Society followed in 1826, trumpeting Rush's theory of the inevitably addictive nature of alcohol. The Washingtonian Temperance Society (named for the first president despite his liberal attitudes toward drink) admitted only "reformed" drinkers to its group. Its membership rolls reached over half a million at their peak. These reformed drinkers either extolled the virtues of quitting drinking by "getting religion," or shifted the blame from their own "sinful" behavior to alcohol itself. The idea that alcohol was the devil — "demon rum" or "spirits" — eventually led to the belief that alcohol was dangerous to *anyone* who drank it, not just to those who drank to intoxication.

On Washington's birthday in 1842, Abraham Lincoln addressed the Springfield Washingtonian Temperance Society, appealing to the members' belief that only those who had been in their shoes could judge them. Lincoln sympathized with the crowd and said that people who preached to and denounced the victims of drink typically had never experienced the problem themselves and only compounded the problem:

> When the dram seller and drinker were incessantly told, not in accents of entreaty and persuasion diffidently addressed by erring man to an erring brother, but in the thundering tones of anathema and denunciation ... that they were the authors of all the vice and misery and crime in the land, that they were the manufacturers and material of all the

thieves and robbers and murderers that infest the earth, that their houses were the workshops of the devil, and that their persons should be shunned by all the good and virtuous as moral pestilences ... I say when they were told all this and in this way, it is not wonderful that they were slow, very slow, to acknowledge the truth of such denunciations and to join the ranks of their denouncers in a hue and cry against themselves.

Another error, as it seems to me, into which the reformers fell was the position that all habitual drunkards were utterly incorrigible and therefore must be turned adrift and damned without remedy in order that the grace of temperance might abound, to the temperate then, and to all mankind some hundreds of years thereafter ... .

In my judgment, such of us as who have never fallen victims have been spared more by the absence of appetite than from any mental or moral superiority over those who have ... . There seems ever to have been a proneness in the brilliant and warm-blooded to fall into this vice. The demon of intemperance ever seems to have delighted in sucking the blood of genius and of generosity ... .

Happy day when all appetites controlled, all poisons subdued, all matter subjected. Mind, all conquering mind, shall live and move the monarch of the world ... .[5]

Despite early disease theories, temperance was largely a moral issue. In the first half of the nineteenth century, the popularity of Protestant revivals mirrored the expansion of temperance meetings. Revivalists encouraged attendees to confess their sins publicly to be saved. As drinkers flocked to them, these revivals became an important mouthpiece of the temperance movement. Temperance activists borrowed revivalist techniques, for instance, by featuring new converts taking public pledges to be temperate. For members who had taken "the total pledge" (or "long pledge") of abstinence, the registrar marked a "T" next to their names, hence the term "teetotaler." (The person who took the "short pledge" still enjoyed beer and wine.) It is estimated that by 1840 nearly 1.5 million Americans were associated with temperance groups.

Although temperance workers were amenable to the disease concept and were sympathetic to those who suffered from chronic inebriation, by the mid-1800s they had directed their message at the casual, moderate drinker in an effort to bring about prohibition of all alcoholic beverages. In fact, by the mid-century, most middle-class Americans had become temperate. In the 1850s a handful of states passed prohibition laws, most of which were quickly repealed by 1860 as the politics of abolition took center stage.

In the mid-1870s, the influential Woman's Christian Temperance Union (WCTU) joined the struggling Prohibitionist party. In return for the WCTU's support, the Prohibitionists added women's suffrage to their party's platform.

Meanwhile, among citizens, the issue of prohibition divided religious groups. According to Professor Pegram,

Christians coming from evangelical or pietistic confessional traditions that laid stress on individual conduct — Methodists,

Congregationalists, Presbyterians, most Baptists, Scandinavian Lutherans, and most smaller Protestant denominations — tended to back prohibition and oppose tax support for Catholic schools and the relaxed Continental Sunday. Those whose faith stressed church traditions and liturgical richness — primarily Catholics, German Lutherans, and Epis-copalians — often interpreted Sunday blue laws and liquor regulations as outrageous restrictions on personal freedom and cultural traditions.[6]

Amending Our Ways

In the mid-1890s, the prominent Anti-Saloon League of America focused its attention on the source of drink rather than on the drinker. The liquor industry became the target of regulations and taxation, and the saloons became a target of protestors. One of the most militant reformers to focus on the saloons was Carry Nation, who swung her hatchet through several Kansas bars in 1900. Most Americans were turned off by the violence, so the majority of reformers chose more respectable means of persuasion.

They were helped, on the eve of Prohibition, by the American Medical Association, which formally con-demned the use of alcohol as a beverage. Doctors based this opinion on, among other things, insurance studies showing higher mortality rates for drinkers than for non-drinkers.

In 1919, the states ratified the Eighteenth Amendment outlawing the production, sale, and trans-portation of "intoxicating liquors." The subsequent

Volstead Act, named for a Minnesota senator, established the means for enforcing Prohibition. Oddly,
instead of the Justice Department, it was the Treasury
Department's Internal Revenue Service that was
charged with enforcing Prohibition. The IRS's lack of
resources (and lack of tax revenue from newly prohib-
ited liquor sales) may have contributed to overall
enforcement problems. Another factor was the reluc-
tance of juries to convict alleged bootleggers, a sign that
temperance was not as widely regarded a virtue as
politicians had thought.

During Prohibition, research into the nature of
chronic inebriation as a disease effectively ceased.
Inebriation, of course, did not. Although total alcohol
consumption did decline during Prohibition, alcoholism
did not disappear, and, in fact, "the whole point of going
out to drink illegal and expensive liquor was to get
drunk."[7]

Furthermore, many new social problems emerged:
bootlegging, organized crime, and their attendant violence. Prohibition became very unpopular, and in 1933
the Twenty-First Amendment repealed it without much
controversy, even from women. (The rise of speakeasies
during Prohibition had the effect of actually drawing
women into the drinking culture. Restaurants and
nightclubs that sold alcohol illegally attracted more
women than had traditional saloons and became places
where the wealthier men and women of the roaring
twenties could meet.) Politics at the time focused on the
state of the economy, which was sinking into the Great
Depression, and the repeal of Prohibition seemed to
promise new jobs and new tax revenue.

Although all states ratified the Twenty-First
Amendment, state prohibition survived in Kansas until
1948, Oklahoma until 1957, and Mississippi until

1966. Largely Mormon Utah is still a dry state, and dry counties can be found in several southern states.

Professor Pegram sums up the temperance movement from its birth to the failure of Prohibition thus:

> From its origins in the nineteenth century, temperance reform had developed as a forward-looking, optimistic social movement. Its proponents had been modernizers, those who looked forward to social, economic, and moral improvement. That image became badly tarnished in the 1920s as prohibition came to be labeled the creaky obsession of puritanical moralists, rural busybodies, and religious bigots. One of the most damaging blows to the reform image of prohibition was the dry enthusiasm exhibited by the hooded knights of the resurgent Ku Klux Klan ... .[8]

That drinking was seen as a largely moral issue, rather than one of public health, is reflected in the fact that most Americans today regard the lesson of Prohibition to be the danger of trying to legislate morality.

Step by Step

In the wake of Prohibition, anyone decrying the dangers of drink was highly unpopular. Medical attention to the nature and treatment of chronic inebriation had dried up, and the public saw intoxication as a personal matter. Problem drinkers seemed to have nowhere to turn, until two men turned to one another in 1935 and Alcoholics Anonymous was born.

Like the Washingtonians, AA admitted only problem drinkers to its membership and based its famed twelve steps in Protestant spirituality. The aspect of public confession ("My name is Bill W., and I'm an alcoholic ... ") is borrowed from nineteenth century revivalism. As Stanton Peele, author of *Diseasing of America*, has pointed out, "The public confessional and repentance, the spiritual rebirth leading to a new identity, and the need to convert others are all part of AA's fundamentalist religious roots."[9]

While spiritually the AA member may be "born again," he or she can never be physically recovered. AA members refer to themselves as "recovering" alcoholics, not "recovered," even after decades of abstinence. According to AA's Big Book, they base this self-image of being permanently diseased on the belief that they suffer from a lifelong, irreversible "allergy" to alcohol. They use this medical hypothesis to distinguish themselves from "normal drinkers." (The methods and effectiveness of AA are discussed in Chapter 7.)

Teetotalers and temperance advocates, meanwhile, were devastated by the failure of Prohibition. Overwhelming public support for alcohol consumption forced them to shift their focus from the moderate drinker to the excessive drinker. Worried that the repeal of Prohibition would spell a return to the harsh punishment of, or public moralizing against, alcoholics, the regrouped temperance faithful looked to the disease concept to help get these people "a better deal" than prison or public humiliation.

The temperate took a lesson from the growing field of psychiatry. Before Freud, "lunatics" were treated with disgust. They were often beaten and incarcerated. Much like drunkards, they were often thought to be evil or possessed by the devil.

Freud said, in effect, that these people are not evil; they are mentally ill. They can be treated, and they deserve facilities designed specifically for their welfare. From the public they deserve compassion. So, too, reasoned temperance adherents, should alcoholics be regarded — as ill, as deserving specific institutions for their treatment.

This position required more public — and medical — acceptance of a disease concept of alcoholism. The medical support came from a series of landmark articles by Dr. Elvin M. Jellinek, who in the 1940s laid the foundation of our modern concept of alcoholism.

•

The Dry Climate

Temperance politics of the 1800s gave rise to many folk songs that emphasized the evils of alcohol and the immorality of falling prey to it. Typical song titles included *Touch Not the Cup* and *Touch It? Not I:*

In the wine cup there is sorrow;
    In its dregs the demons lie,
Now so bright, 'tis black tomorrow;
    Touch it? Not I;
Touch it? Not I; Touch it? Not I;
    In its very breath is poison;
    Touch it? Not I.[10]

Touch Not, Taste Not, Handle Not, by the Reverend Dwight Williams, had a more urgent appeal:

There's a danger in the flowing bowl!
Touch not, taste not, handle not!
'Twill ruin body, ruin soul!
Touch not, taste not, handle not!
'Twill rob the pocket of its cash;
'Twill scourge thee with a cruel lash;
And all thy hopes of pleasure dash,
Touch not, taste not, handle not!

"Strong drink is raging," God hath
    said:
Touch not, taste not, handle not!
And thousands it hath captive led!
Touch not, taste not, handle not!
It leads the young and strong and
    brave;
It leads them to a drunkard's grave
It leads them where no arm can
    save —
Touch not, taste not, handle not!

Come, let us join each heart and
    hand
Touch not, taste not, handle not!
To drive the traffic from the land;
Touch not, taste not, handle not!
We need the strongest, bravest
    hearts
To foil the cruel tempter's arts,
And heal his fearful wounds and
    smarts, —
Touch not, taste not, handle not!

Oh, hasten, then, the happy time!
Touch not, taste not, handle not!

We'll ring the bells with joyous
  chime;
Touch not, taste not, handle not!
We'll raise the temp'rance flag on
  high,
And lift our voices to the sky —
Sing, glory be to God on high, —
Touch not, taste not, handle not!

Songs that were in essence rallying cries for the movement included "The Ship of Temperance" and at least two songs entitled "Marching on to Victory."

Even *America the Beautiful*, written by Katherine Lee Bates and Samuel A. Ward in 1895 during an upswing in temperance sentiment, contains some lyrics that may refer to temperance as much as to self-governance: "America, America / God mend thy every flaw, / Confirm thy soul / In self-control, / Thy liberty in law." (Perhaps it's more appropriate, if not a little ironic, that the melody of the song chosen as our national anthem, *The Star-Spangled Banner*, was based on the eighteenth-century British drinking song *To Anacreon, in Heaven*.)

Songwriters weren't the only members of the arts community to weigh in on the temperance debate. During the mid-1800s, like today, it was commonplace for writers, poets, and artists to take opium or drink alcohol to get their creative juices flowing. American essayist Ralph Waldo Emerson opined on this practice, claiming inebriation thus attained did not provide the poet with "true" vision:

The poet knows that he speaks adequately ... only when he speaks somewhat wildly, or "with the flower of the mind"; not with the intellect used as an organ, but with the intellect released from all service and suffered to take its direction from its celestial life; or as the ancients were wont to express themselves, not with intellect alone but with the intellect inebriated by nectar ... . For if in any manner we can stimulate this instinct, new passages are opened for us into nature; the mind flows into and through things hardest and highest, and the metamorphosis is possible.

This is the reason why bards love wine, mead, narcotics, coffee, tea, opium, the fumes of sandalwood and tobacco, or whatever other procurers of animal exhilaration ... [But these are] substitutes for the true nectar, which is the ravishment of the intellect by coming nearer to the fact ... . But never can any advantage be taken of nature by trick. The spirit of the world, the great calm presence of the Creator, comes not forth to the sorceries of opium or of wine. The sublime vision comes to the pure and simple soul in a clean and chaste body ... .[11]

•

3 The Diseased Drinker

*"First you take a drink, then the drink takes a drink,
then the drink takes you."*
–F. Scott Fitzgerald

IN THE MID-1940s and early 1950s, Elvin M. Jellinek, a research professor at the Yale Center for Alcohol Studies, wrote two well-received articles that proposed both a scientific framework from which to understand alcohol problems and an argument for treating them medically.[1]

Based on questionnaires given to AA members, Jellinek's conception of alcoholism as a progressive disease, not surprisingly, mirrored the AA view: the alcoholic's social drinking gradually increased until he eventually lost control over the amount of alcohol he consumed once he began drinking. The drinker's control deteriorated until he hit "rock bottom," where he was finally persuaded into abstaining from alcohol. Jellinek's data not only provided support for AA, but attracted enough media attention so that the public began to accept the AA view.

Jellinek followed up his articles with the highly influential book, *The Disease Concept of Alcoholism*, published in 1960.[2] He divided alcoholism into five types:

1. Alpha, characterized by psychological dependence;
2. Beta, characterized by heavy drinking resulting in physical damage but not physical or psychological dependence;
3. Gamma, or "alcohol addiction" consisting of increased tolerance, adaptive metabolism, withdrawal symptoms, craving, and loss of control;
4. Delta, characterized by control over the amount of alcohol drunk, but no ability to abstain; and
5. Epsilon, referring to periodic or "binge" drinking.

Jellinek believed only the gamma and delta versions of alcoholism, which manifested symptoms of physical dependence, qualified as the disease.

No corroborative evidence was ever produced to support five distinct forms of alcoholism, and the usefulness of distinguishing five types has subsequently been rejected. The medical establishment, however, came to accept a combination of the gamma and delta explanations of alcoholism as a disease.

The primary criteria for this definition were thus seen as loss of control and craving. Jellinek was tentative about defining "loss of control"; he was reluctant to say, as adherents to AA theories did (and still do), that loss of control always follows the first drink. In merely citing AA members' beliefs about the instantaneous and inevitable loss of control, however, Jellinek gave credence to them. As philosopher Herbert Fingarette points out in his book *Heavy Drinking*: "Despite his own scholarly reservations and nuances, [Jellinek's] work had the practical effect of reinforcing the AA colloquial axiom, 'one drink, one drunk,' and of encouraging people to speak of alcoholics as driven to drink by an 'overwhelming desire,' an 'irresistible craving,' or a 'compulsion.' Thus the 'folk science' of alcoholism was propagated."[3]

Furthermore, although Jellinek's book did not go so far as to say that alcoholism was irreversible or that permanent abstinence was the necessary treatment, AA advocates of permanent abstinence often refer to his book in citing support for their position.[4] In fact, Jellinek never intended his articles or his book to be taken as the definitive text on alcoholism. He emphasized that researchers should use his hypotheses as the basis for empirical scientific studies to confirm or deny their validity: " ... acceptance of certain formulations on the nature of alcoholism does not necessarily equal validity. I am repeating these words at this juncture lest there should be some misunderstanding on this score."[5]

As Jellinek was devising his disease theory, one of the first female members of AA, Marty Mann, a professional publicist, created the National Council on Alcoholism (NCA). The mission of this nonprofit organization was to persuade Americans that alcoholism was a disease, that alcoholics were sick people in need of treatment, and that alcoholism was a pervasive public health problem. Although AA, as a rule, takes no official position on any external medical or scientific claim, the NCA effectively worked to promote the AA philosophy to the American public.

Largely owing to the work of Jellinek and the publicity the NCA generated for it, the World Health Organization drafted the following definition of alcoholism as a disease in 1952:

> Alcoholics are those excessive drinkers whose dependence on alcohol has attained such a degree that it shows a noticeable mental disturbance or an interference with their bodily and mental health, their personal rela-

tions and their smooth economic functioning, or who show the prodromal signs of such development. They therefore need treatment.[6]

The definition left much room for interpretation, especially for the terms "excessive," "noticeable," and "smooth," and contained no definition of the word "dependence." Objective criteria by which to diagnose the disease was therefore lacking. Despite such ambiguities, in 1956 the American Medical Association nevertheless accepted alcoholism as a disease that doctors were responsible for treating.

The Progression of Disease Theories

Jellinek's work inspired other scientists to conduct experiments, surveys, and other research to confirm his disease theory and its components, uncover the causes of the disease, and, ultimately, develop a cure. Despite the fact that much of this research tended to disprove the notions of loss of control and irreversibility (discussed in Chapter 4), the NCA managed to propagate the disease perspective. In time, more refined disease theories emerged. In their book *Problem Drinking*, research psychologists Nick Heather and Ian Robertson classify them thus:
1. Alcoholism as pre-existent physical abnormality
2. Alcoholism as mental illness or psychopathology
3. Alcoholism as acquired addiction or dependence[7]
Pre-existent physical abnormality. In this theory, the disease is something the alcoholic is born with. AA's original allergy theory corresponds to this view. While scientists have dismissed an "allergy" per se as a cause, they have conducted extensive research into

the differences in the ways in which individuals metabolize alcohol, as well as into the genetic roots of such metabolism.

Alcohol is processed in the liver, which converts it first to acetaldehyde, a highly toxic chemical, and then to acetate. Some people's liver enzymes convert alcohol into acetaldehyde at a much faster rate (up to forty times faster), or at a significantly slower rate, than do others'. As a result, the toxic acetaldehyde stays in these people's bodies longer. This could account for an unpleasant physical reaction to alcohol, or, in some cases, possibly a more pleasant reaction. In either case, these extreme metabolic rates are thought to be a risk factor for becoming alcoholic.

Members of certain ethnic groups, including Eskimos, Native Americans, Chinese, and Japanese, tend to metabolize alcohol at these extreme rates, which accounts for the facial reddening ("flushing"), nausea, and rapid heartbeat they experience when they drink. In the United States, however, Eskimos and Native Americans have the highest rates of alcoholism among ethnic groups, while Chinese and Japanese have the lowest. Such differences tend to point to cultural factors outweighing metabolic factors in determining the risk for becoming alcoholic.

The metabolic processes described above are largely under genetic control. Since 1990, when scientists began to make great strides in genetic research, studies have investigated not only how genes direct the actions of liver enzymes, but also how they affect brain chemicals that may be particularly sensitive to alcohol. Identifying specific genes, or the interaction of specific genes, that contribute to a predisposition toward alcoholism is slow-going. So far, only a few genes have been identified. Specifically, defective versions of the genes

ALDH2, ADH2, and ADH3, common among Asians, determines the action of the liver enzyme responsible for metabolizing alcohol.

A recent article in the *Journal of the American Medical Association* by Marc A. Schuckit of the University of California School of Medicine, a leading researcher in this field, suggested that some people might carry a genetic predisposition in their brain chemistry, specifically with regard to (a) dopamine, which neurologically transmits the pleasurable sensations of alcohol and other drugs, and (b) endogenous opioids, which stimulate pleasurable feelings and suppress pain.[8]

How important are genes in determining a person's risk for alcoholism? To precisely quantify the magnitude of genetic influence, scientists would have to do the impossible — that is, conduct experiments in which they can completely remove environmental factors from consideration. One notable study, however, came as close as possible. In 1974, Donald Goodwin and his colleagues examined the sons of alcoholic parents who had put their children up for adoption. Their sons' adoptive parents were not themselves alcoholics, thus diminishing the environmental effects that could have influenced the children. These sons were compared with adoptee sons whose natural parents were not alcoholics. The sons whose natural parents were alcoholics were almost four times more likely to become alcoholics than the sons of non-alcoholic parents.[9]

Although this is certainly a statistically significant increase in risk, it by no means represents an inevitability. When the results are put another way, 20 percent of the sons of an alcoholic parent become alcoholics, but 80 percent don't.[10]

Similar studies involving the daughters of alcoholics

revealed no such increased likelihood of alcoholism, which dashes hopes for a straightforward genetic explanation.

Other genetic studies conducted in the 1960s examined the likelihood that when one twin is an alcoholic, the other one will be as well. Studies have indeed shown a concordance rate of approximately 70 percent; in other words, when one twin was an alcoholic, the other was also an alcoholic in 70 percent of the cases.[11]

This concordance rate between identical twins was compared to the concordance rate between fraternal twins, which was lower. Because identical twins have identical genetic make-up and fraternal twins are no more alike genetically than regular siblings, a greater concurrence of alcoholism among identical twins than among fraternal twins confirms the presence of genetic risk factors.

In its Introduction to the *Tenth Annual Report to Congress*, published in 1999, the National Institute for Alcohol Abuse and Alcoholism (NIAAA) asserts, "Today we know that approximately 50 to 60 percent of the risk for developing alcoholism is genetic." Obviously, not everyone who carries the defective genes becomes an alcoholic, and certainly someone who does not carry the genes can become alcoholic as a result of other environmental factors. The NIAAA report puts its high risk rate into perspective by explaining that "future research ... will require understanding all the component [genetic] parts as a system that does not preordain behavior, but to some degree sets the stage."[12]

What are the hopes for future genetic research? Although scientists no longer expect to discover a single gene that causes alcoholism, they continue to study the multiple genetic factors for three reasons: (1) to develop screening tests for people who want to assess their risk for becoming alcoholic, (2) to develop genetic engineering techniques to "disable" the defective genes; and (3) to develop drugs that will counteract genetically controlled metabolic processes. All such goals have their limitations. Is it truly helpful, for instance, for someone who learns he has a genetic risk factor for alcoholism to fear liquor and abstain from alcohol at all costs? (A similar debate surrounds the discovery of the "breast cancer" gene — should a woman with the gene undergo major surgery to remove her breasts before developing any signs of breast cancer?) Genetic engineering raises a host of ethical issues, not the least of which is how an "engineered" person will pass along altered genes to his or her children. Finally, while the prospect of developing a pill to cure any ailment naturally generates lots of excitement, the ultimate cost, benefit, or usefulness of drug treatment is up for debate. Diagnosed alcoholics can already be treated with the highly effective drug Antabuse (discussed in Chapter 7), but success depends entirely on getting them to take their medicine.

Because the field of genetic research is relatively new, the public may get the impression that it will eventually yield cures for whatever ails us — including, for instance, baldness, premenstrual syndrome, menopause, and obesity. That these conditions are controlled largely, if not totally, by genes is not necessarily sufficient reason for us to regard them as diseases. If, for example, we think of menopause, a natural process of female aging, as a disease, then it is a short leap to think of being female as a disease. This is not to say that women should not seek to relieve the uncomfortable effects of menopause or PMS, but that it would not be beneficial or useful for them to see themselves as diseased people. So, too, people debate whether the fact that alcoholism may be partly influenced by genetic factors is sufficient reason to call alcoholism a disease. (Chapter 6 explores this debate more fully.) When considering treatment, however, one should keep genetic research in perspective, as environmental factors are at least as important as genetic factors in the development of alcoholism. In *Problem Drinking*, authors Nick Heather and Ian Robertson write:

> ... in the alcohol field, the new popularity of genetic explanations has also been supported by a massive expansion, particularly in the USA, of research funding for this type of work. It is not unreasonable to suggest that this research expansion has been based partly on ideological rather than strict scientific grounds; it is far more convenient for governments, particularly those of a right-wing bent, to ascribe problems due to drinking to the vulnerabilities of those individuals who suffer from such problems rather than to social and environmental factors for which they might be held responsible. Be that as it may, one wonders what progress could have been made in identifying the psychological, social and cultural causes of problem drinking had a similar increase in research funding occurred there too.[13]

In *The Natural History of Alcoholism Revisited*, Harvard researcher George E. Vaillant also cautions against focusing too narrowly on genetics when studying alcoholism: "What is needed is not an argument that one or another factor is the most important cause of the development of alcoholism, but rather an effort to understand the relative etiological contributions of each variable to the total clinical picture."[14]

Mental illness or psychopathology. The idea that the cause of alcoholism could be due to psychological factors alone goes back to Freud. Theories have attributed alcoholism to an inferiority complex, abnormally heavy dependence on one's mother, repressed homosexuality, an unconscious desire for self-destruction, and so on. There seem to be as many psychological theories as there are alcoholics. Indeed, attempts at creating a profile of "the alcoholic personality" have been thwarted by individual differences.

Acquired addiction or dependence. In this view, the disease does not exist before the person starts drinking. Put another way, anyone who tries hard enough can become an alcoholic.[15]

In 1976, Griffith Edwards and his colleagues introduced the term "alcohol dependence syndrome" to replace "alcoholism." They defined the syndrome as a "psycho-physiological disorder" containing the following seven elements:

1. Narrowing of the drinking repertoire (a predictable pattern of drinking)
2. Salience of drink-seeking behavior (preoccupation with drinking, to the exclusion of other activities)
3. Increased tolerance to alcohol (the ability to function while maintaining blood alcohol levels that would incapacitate the non-tolerant drinker)
4. Repeated withdrawal symptoms (primarily shaking, sweating, nausea, and mood swings)
5. Subjective awareness of a compulsion to drink (realizing the desire for further drink is irrational, but drinking anyway)
6. Relief or avoidance of withdrawal symptoms by further drinking

7. Reinstatement of dependence after abstinence[16]

This progression implies that without treatment, the alcoholic will continue to deteriorate and is likely, in the absence of a fatal accident, to eventually die due to alcohol-related organ damage. While this explanation differs from AA's view that the alcoholic is born "different" or "diseased," it does support AA's notion of the irreversibility of alcoholism.

The syndrome conception of problem drinking came as the biggest challenge to Jellinek's original theory. Although it has since been criticized (Chapter 4 examines popular beliefs about the nature of addiction and the scientific evidence supporting or contradicting them), the World Health Organization subsequently dropped the term "alcoholism" from the *International Classification of Diseases* and replaced it with "alcohol dependence syndrome."

All of the above disease theories have contributed to our current beliefs about alcoholism, even though the word itself is no longer used by medical authorities. *The Diagnostic and Statistical Manual of Mental Disorders* (DSM-IV, 1994) replaced the medical diagnosis "alcoholism" with two others: "alcohol dependence" and "alcohol abuse." "Alcohol dependence" is characterized by cognitive behavioral and often physical symptoms, including tolerance and withdrawal, although "physiological dependence" does not have to be present in cases in which the individual has impaired control of alcohol use and continues use of alcohol despite adverse consequences. "Alcohol abuse" is characterized by harmful patterns of alcohol use that have never met the criteria for dependence, including recurrent use of alcohol in situations when use is physically dangerous (e.g., driving while intoxicated).[17]

Despite these carefully worded diagnostic criteria,

the National Council on Alcoholism and Drug Dependence (an expansion of the original NCA) and the American Council on Alcoholism, a nonprofit organization, promote the following greatly expanded definition of alcoholism, with a careful consideration of their terms:

> Alcoholism is a primary, chronic disease with genetic, psychosocial, and environmental factors influencing its development and manifestations. The disease is often progressive and fatal. It is characterized by continuous or periodic: impaired control over drinking, preoccupation with the drug alcohol, use of alcohol despite adverse consequences, and distortions in thinking, most notably denial.
>
> "Primary" refers to the nature of alcoholism as a disease entity in addition to and separate from other pathophysiologic states which may be associated with it. "Primary" suggests that alcoholism, as an addiction, is not a symptom of an underlying disease state.
>
> "Disease" means an involuntary disability. It represents the sum of the abnormal phenomena displayed by a group of individuals. These phenomena are associated with a specified common set of characteristics by which these individuals differ from the norm, and which places them at a disadvantage.
>
> "Often progressive and fatal" means that the disease persists over time and that physical, emotional, and social changes are often cumulative and may progress as drinking continues. Alcoholism causes premature death through overdose, organic complications

involving the brain, liver, heart and many other organs, and by contributing to suicide, homicide, motor vehicle crashes, and other traumatic events.

"Impaired control" means the inability to limit alcohol use or to consistently limit on any drinking occasion the duration of the episode, the quantity consumed, and/or the behavioral consequences of drinking.

"Preoccupation" in association with alcohol use indicates excessive, focused attention given to the drug alcohol, its effects, and/or its use. The relative value thus assigned to alcohol by the individual often leads to a diversion of energies away from important life concerns.

"Adverse consequences" are alcohol-related problems or impairments in such areas as: physical health (e.g., alcohol withdrawal syndromes, liver disease, gastritis, anemia, neurological disorders); psychological functioning (e.g., impairments in cognition, changes in mood and behavior); interpersonal functioning (e.g., marital problems and child abuse, impaired social relationships); occupational functioning (e.g., scholastic or job problems); and legal, financial, or spiritual problems.

"Denial" is used here not only in the psychoanalytic sense of a single psychological defense mechanism disavowing the significance of events, but more broadly to include a range of psychological maneuvers designed to reduce awareness of the fact that alcohol use is the cause of an individual's problems rather than a solution to those problems. Denial becomes an integral part of the disease and a major obstacle to recovery.

This disease definition is the one that the American public is most familiar with; however, it is not the one accepted by research authorities. Chapter 4 investigates why.

•

"Guinness Is Good For You"

Medicine and the media have not always taken a harsh attitude toward alcohol. It was often seen as an elixir, a tonic, a remedy. Doctors prescribed hot rum toddies for colds; whiskey was rubbed on the gums of teething children to numb their pain. And, as cigarettes were initially marketed to the public as contributing to a healthy lifestyle, so too was alcohol sold for its alleged health benefits. In 1929, for instance, the first ad for Guinness proclaimed its "health giving values" and "nourishing properties":

Guinness builds strong muscles. It feeds exhausted nerves. It enriches the blood. Doctors affirm that Guinness is a valuable restorative after Influenza and other weakening sicknesses. Guinness is a valuable natural aid in cases of insomnia ... . Guinness is one of the most nourishing beverages, richer in carbohydrates than a glass of milk. That is one reason why it is so good when people are tired or exhausted. Guinness is Good for You.

Indeed, English doctors used to give Guinness to patients recovering from surgery as well as to blood donors. In Ireland, it is still given to blood donors and those recovering from digestive disorders, as Guinness has a high iron content. (Presumably Guinness is more abundant in Ireland than other iron-rich foods like onions and leafy green vegetables.) However, the beverage is not, as some ads led people to believe, high in "vitamin G."

Alcohol is still a common ingredient in many over-the-counter cold and flu remedies, as well as in numerous prescription medications. Alcohol treatment centers often confiscate all such products when admitting new patients into rehab, in the belief that even the slightest bit of cherry-flavored cough syrup can push a recovering alcoholic off the wagon.

Scientists still believe that moderate amounts of alcohol can, in fact, be good for you. In the past twenty years researchers have discovered substances in red wine that supposedly protect against heart disease, thus accounting for the low rates of heart disease among the French and in other countries whose citizens prefer grape-based beverages. Other studies have found that having no more than one drink a day may offer some protection against certain forms of cancer or reduce the risk of stroke. Despite such studies, however, no one expects the USDA to add "the alcohol group" to its pyramid of dietary recommendations any time soon.

•

4 Why the Disease Theory Won't Hold Water

"Wine hath drowned more Men than the Sea."
–Thomas Fuller, *Gnomologia: Adages and Proverbs*

ALL OF THE classic disease theories of alcoholism hang their hats on the presence of one or more of the following factors: irreversibility, progression of increasing alcohol consumption and physical deterioration, loss of control, craving, and physical dependence. Researchers have demonstrated, however, that these factors are not always or significantly at play in people diagnosed as alcoholics.

No Going Back?

The idea of irreversibility was propagated, most successfully, by Alcoholics Anonymous with the following catchphrases: "Once an alcoholic, always an alcoholic," "always recovering, never recovered," and "one drink, one drunk." As it was thought that even a drop of alcohol could send the sober alcoholic off on a bender from which he might never recover, treatment for alcoholism necessarily involved total abstinence.

Dr. D.L. Davies challenged that notion in his 1962

report that followed up on diagnosed "alcohol addicts" who had been treated in a London hospital seven to ten years earlier.[1] Follow-up sources included the patients' outpatient records, social worker contact, and correspondence with relatives. Dr. Davies noted in his report that seven out of the ninety-three male patients seemed to be drinking normally. He did not define "normal," noting only that some of these patients drank up to three pints of beer a day; others drank only on holidays.

To say that response to Dr. Davies' finding was avid and critical is an understatement. Experts in the field sent commentaries to the *Quarterly Journal of Studies on Alcohol* questioning whether the seven "normal" drinkers were ever "true" alcoholics. The WHO definition of alcoholism, used to diagnose the patients originally, was called into question. Other critics warned that the normal drinkers were heading for an inevitable relapse. Some attributed the finding to a "freak" instance of spontaneous remission, nothing significant enough to change the standard treatment goal of abstinence. While Davies had suggested no such alteration in treatment, experts worried that abstinent alcoholics would get wind of the report and begin drinking again to test whether they, like the seven Davies patients, safely could.

In response, Dr. Davies argued that the potential for the press to publicize reports in scientific journals out of context in a manner that might have unintentional negative consequences is never a justification for suppressing clinical findings. Shortly after the Davies report, another scientist reporting safe drinking among diagnosed alcoholics claimed he was practically ordered by the organization that had funded his research to omit these "embarrassing" findings.[2]

In fact, reports of normal drinking among former alcoholics had been observed by researchers long before Dr. Davies' controversial report. Their findings had largely been small notes in broad studies and buried among other findings. In most of these cases, the researchers were not looking for normal drinking outcomes; the normal drinking findings they reported were unexpected. Nonetheless, normal drinking outcomes were being reported even as the notion of irreversibility was becoming widely accepted. (A brief summary of these reports appears on pages 56–58.)

Furthermore, researchers have identified nearly eighty studies that had been published in the scientific literature prior to 1980 demonstrating that non-problem drinking is a stable treatment outcome.[3] These studies reported rates of observed normal drinking among previously diagnosed alcoholics varying between 2 and 32 percent. The authors of *Problem Drinking* point out that "proponents of the disease perspective sometimes give the impression that normal drinking in former alcoholics is something which has only just been dreamt up by naïve and inexperienced researchers. Nothing could be farther from the truth and this particular inadequacy of the disease theory became obvious from the first introduction of scientific methods in the field."[4]

"Normal Drinking" Observed in Formerly Diagnosed Alcoholics

The following list, which is by no means exhaustive, summarizes some of the early reports of normal drinking in former alcoholics from 1955 to 1972. (For more detailed information about, and a critique of, each one, and for citations to the original reports, see Chapter 2 of Nick Heather and Ian Robertson's 1981 book *Controlled Drinking*, published by Methuen.)

Bear in mind that scientific methods improved greatly over these years, so many of the early (primarily 1950s) reports may be flawed. Some information may have been collected by relying only on the subjects' "self-reports," for instance, rather than on corroborative evidence obtained from friends, relatives, employers, physicians, and social workers. In addition, ideas about what constitutes "normal drinking" could vary significantly. In many cases, the researchers did not define exactly what they meant by it, using terms like "problem-free," "occasional," "moderate," and "social," but not specifying precise amounts.

1952: In France, researchers studied 500 cases of patients treated for alcoholism five years earlier. Roughly 15 percent were drinking socially. The researchers presumed they drank primarily to keep up appearances in the wine-drinking French culture.

1953: A study of the histories of 500 deceased alcoholics revealed that 10 percent had been drinking moderately and problem-free for several years before their deaths.

1954: A psychotherapist chronicled a formerly alcoholic client's successful return to moderate drinking after a five-year abstinence.

1956: A three- to five-year follow-up study of patients who had been treated for alcoholism in a Copenhagen hospital revealed that roughly 50 percent drank moderately at special occasions, compared to less than 30 percent who were completely abstinent.

1957: Of sixty British alcoholics whose employers referred them to outpatient treatment, 12 percent established problem-free, moderate drinking patterns one year later.

1960: Alcoholic veterans who received psychotherapy were followed up between one and six years after treatment. Of 100, 23 percent had reduced their drinking and 15 percent were abstinent. The study went on to evaluate the men by the quality of their overall behavior, marital relationships, and other social and medical factors. Of the fourteen most improved patients, five were "well-controlled social drinkers," which suggests that abstinence is not a prerequisite for overall life improvement.

1965: Among sixty-two people whose physicians had referred them to a hospital for alcoholism treatment, but who were never treated, four managed to reduce their drinking to harm-free levels for at least three years.

1967: In New York, roughly 10 percent of

ninety-one questionnaire respondents who had reported previous drinking problems were found to be drinking in a normal manner several years later.

1968: One year after inpatient treatment, four of 156 alcoholic patients had resumed occasional, harm-free social drinking.

1968: Twenty-three percent of eighty-eight alcoholics were drinking moderately one year after hospital treatment; 25 percent were abstaining.

1969: In a twenty-six-month follow-up, three of seventy-six male patients treated for alcoholism resumed social drinking without deterioration.

1971: Two studies confirmed that two of eighty-five and three of twenty alcoholics, respectively, had returned to drinking moderately.

1971: Ninety-three alcoholics were followed up eight years after their release from prison. Seven were found to be abstaining; seventeen were drinking moderately, rarely becoming intoxicated; and eight drank heavily only one night a week, having experienced no drink-related legal, employment, or health problems for at least two years.

1972: Twenty-four of forty-five female alcoholics treated in a psychiatric hospital showed good outcomes one year later; of these, almost half (eleven) had returned to problem-free, moderate drinking.

One of the most public controversies involving former alcoholics' moderate drinking involved a government-commissioned report. In 1970, President Nixon signed a bill creating the National Institute on Alcohol Abuse and Alcoholism (NIAAA). Among its duties was to create and monitor the effectiveness of a number of alcoholism treatment centers nationwide. After several years, the government commissioned the Rand Corporation, an independent nonprofit organization that provides research and analysis on matters relating to public policy, to collect and analyze all the data regarding treatment that these NIAAA-affiliated centers produced between 1970 and 1974. At the time the largest follow-up study of treated alcoholics, the so-called Rand Report was based on interviews of 2,339 male alcoholics six months after treatment and 589 eighteen months later.[5]

In summarizing their findings, the Rand researchers wrote that the data suggest "the possibility that for some alcoholics, moderate drinking is not necessarily a prelude to a full relapse and that some alcoholics can return to moderate drinking with no greater chance of relapse than if they had abstained."

The press got hold of the Rand Report before experts had a chance to review it, sparking a lively controversy. The National Council on Alcoholism, whose mission reflected AA dogma, publicly denounced the report as "dangerous" and "unscientific" before it had even received a copy of it.[6] Many people even suggested that the government should have suppressed the report.

The most famous long-term study of the progressive course of alcoholism is George E. Vaillant's *The Natural History of Alcoholism*, published in 1983 and revised in 1995. "Natural history," Dr. Vaillant explains, is the development of the individual's physical reactivity to alcohol abuse; it does not refer to a person's style of drinking or to environmental or social factors. Natural history implies only a "biological condition with a tendency, once established, toward an inexorable progression of symptoms."[7]

Dr. Vaillant's book analyzes data from Harvard Medical School's Study of Adult Development, which followed 660 men from 1940 to 1980, from their adolescence into late middle age. Researchers collected information about many aspects of the men's lives, including their drinking. The men were selected from two groups: 204 sophomores at an elite college and 456 teenagers from a less-privileged inner-city environment. The data about these men's lives were compared with information from a sample of 100 alcohol-dependent men and women followed for fourteen years after being admitted to a clinic for detoxification.

Of all the college and inner-city subjects, roughly 25 percent met the diagnostic criteria for alcohol abuse at some point in their lives. Most of the inner-city alcohol abusers developed their drinking problems before the age of 40, while the college alcohol abusers tended to develop their problems after the age of 40. In fact, the alcohol abuse among the college-age men turned out to be a very poor predictor of heavy drinking at middle age. This finding supports other studies that have found that most college-age binge drinkers outgrow their heavy drinking behavior once they leave college and begin jobs or start families. Dr. Vaillant points to one such study by K.M. Fillmore, whose follow-up of college students with drinking problems found that only 20 percent still had problems twenty years later. Furthermore, she observed that blackouts in college correlated only .07 percent with severe alcohol problems two decades hence.[8] Dr. Vaillant, approaching his study from the disease perspective of alcoholism, wrote, "The course of alcohol abusers in the college sample contradicted my previous assertions that sustained alcohol abuse without abstinence is a progressive disorder."[9]

Among the Harvard study's college men who were abusing alcohol from age 45 to age 70, their abuse got neither better nor worse; in other words, they did not develop alcohol dependence and had little in common with study participants who were dependent.[10] In fact, the twenty chronic alcohol abusers spent the years between age 47 and 72 "alternating between controlled drinking and a pattern of alcohol abuse that usually caused problems only to their self-esteem and to their family."[11] Dr. Vaillant likened this pattern of alcohol abuse to the pattern of obesity in individuals 50 to 70 years old, rather than to that of a progressive illness like multiple sclerosis.

In reviewing studies of recovery from alcoholism without formal treatment, University of Washington professor of psychology G. Alan Marlatt found that moderation outcomes are prevalent, even for individuals who clearly met the diagnostic (DSM-IV) criteria for alcohol dependence at one time.[12] Dr. Marlatt cites one study in which 75 percent of participants who reported previous drinking problems recovered without formal treatment, and 50 percent achieved stable, moderate drinking habits.[13] He concludes, "Contrary to the progressive disease model, these findings indicate that a majority of individuals with drinking problems recover on their own."[14]

The studies described above fail to support the related theories that (1) alcoholism is irreversible, and (2) that it always follows a course of progressive deterioration. Further analyses of the many studies reporting normal drinking in previously diagnosed alcoholics have led researchers to reach the following conclusions:

- Normal drinking is a stable outcome, at least as stable as abstinence.[15]
- The former alcoholics who had the best chances for successful normal drinking outcomes had had fewer serious drinking problems (e.g., never experiencing the delirium tremens), were younger (their habits were less ingrained), were women (women tend to be more motivated to overcome drinking problems because society in general is not as accepting of alcoholic behavior among females as it is among males), or were formerly incarcerated (a long stretch of forced abstinence may contribute to ex-cons' renewed control).
- Treatment is not a prerequisite for a return to normal drinking.

Uncontrollable Desires

The alcoholic's "loss of control" figures prominently in the classic disease model of alcoholism. Loss of control is the drinker's inability to stop drinking once he has started. Someone observing an alcoholic at a bar would probably swear to recognize the phenomenon of "loss of control." Proving it, however, is more difficult. The trick is to decide whether a person has *physically* lost control or whether he has consciously — or unconsciously — decided not to exercise it. Researchers have devised many ingenious experiments to assess whether a drinker has indeed experienced a physical loss of control following a "priming dose" of alcohol. (Because the earliest of these experiments came under ethical scrutiny for their practice of giving alcohol to alcoholics, the researchers were careful to monitor their fully consenting volunteer subjects at all times and conduct the experiments in well-staffed medical facilities.)

In the late 1960s, experiments at the National Institute of Mental Health in Maryland by Drs. Mendelson and Mello and their colleagues,[16] allowed alcoholics to obtain credits toward the purchase of an ounce of alcohol by turning a switch, pressing a button, or performing a similarly monotonous task according to instructions. Credits for an ounce could be earned in as little as five minutes, depending on the subject's skill in performing the task. The subjects determined when to receive their drinks and how much to be given at a time.

While the subjects could have drunk themselves unconscious at any time, none chose to do so. No subject chose to drink all the alcohol available to him, even when no effort was required to obtain it. The subjects drank to maintain high blood alcohol levels, but did not drink continuously; nor did they always drink immediately when alcohol became available, choosing instead to accumulate alcohol credits; and some chose to eventually taper their drinking to reduce the severity of withdrawal symptoms at the end of the experiment. The amount of alcohol they consumed depended on how much effort they felt like exerting to acquire it. In other words, alcoholic drinking appeared to be "a behavior shaped and maintained by its environmental consequences."[17]

An experiment conducted at Johns Hopkins University in 1971 tried to determine the incentives it would take to get an alcoholic *not* to drink. The researchers allowed their subjects, four male alcoholics, to purchase copious amounts of alcohol; for each of the following several days, they offered each man a certain amount of money to abstain for the entire day. If the subject did not abstain, the monetary incentive was increased the next day. If the subject abstained, the monetary incentive was decreased the next day. The results showed that abstinence could be bought for as little as seven and no more than twenty dollars. Given the right incentive, this experiment shows, an alcoholic can choose not to drink.[18]

Other studies have replicated this finding. In a five-week experiment, inpatient subjects were given the option to drink up to ten ounces of alcohol every week-day. Every other week, the subjects were given access to an improved environment — including telephone, television, pool table, games, and reading materials — provided they drank fewer than five ounces of alcohol for the day. If the subject exceeded that amount, he was put in a more Spartan environment and was not allowed to drink the following day. On the alternate weeks, the subjects remained in ascetic environments no matter how much they drank. All five subjects drank less during the weeks when privileges were available than during the weeks when no privileges were available.[19] In *Controlled Drinking*, the authors critiquing the study conclude: "When given the opportunity to determine the amount and patterning of their own drinking in a laboratory situation, alcoholics do not drink mechanically to extreme degrees of intoxication and do not drink all the alcohol available to them. They do not show inability to stop drinking. Moreover, circumstances can be easily arranged whereby it is possible to elicit abstinence or moderation from alcoholics ... ."[20]

In 1977, a review of scientific literature cited fifty-eight studies that have corroborated the finding that alcoholic drinking is a function of "environmental contingencies."[21]

Other ingenious experiments have tested alcoholics' craving for alcohol in situations where (a) the subjects did not know their beverages contained alcohol, or (b) they thought they were drinking alcohol, but in fact they were not, and vice versa. These experiments attempted to separate psychological craving and control from physiological craving and control.

In 1966 psychiatrist Julius Merry conducted an experiment in which nine inpatients were given what they were told was an orange-juice-flavored vitamin drink at breakfast. For the first two days, the drink contained vodka; for the next two days it did not, alternating this pattern for sixteen days. Shortly after breakfast every day, the subjects were asked, among other things, to rate their degree of craving for alcohol on a five-point scale. There were no differences in average craving ratings between the days when subjects drank the alcoholic beverage and the days they drank the nonalcoholic beverages. Dr. Merry interpreted these results as refuting the idea that small quantities of alcohol trigger a biochemical response resulting in craving. He boldly titled the article reporting his results "The Loss of Control Myth."[22]

In 1972, researchers assigned each of ten alcoholic inpatients to one of four groups. All groups were given a "vitamin" drink for breakfast. Group 1's drink did not contain any alcohol. Group 2's drink contained vodka, but the subjects were not told it contained vodka. Groups 3 and 4 were told their drinks contained alcohol, but in fact, Group 3's did not. Shortly after breakfast, the subjects were given a questionnaire asking them, among other unrelated things, to rate their craving for alcohol. Group 2, which had been given alcohol but had not been so informed, reported the least degree of craving. Group 3, which had been given alcohol and had been informed, reported the highest degree of craving. The results of this test seem to indicate that an alcoholic's desire for alcohol increases when he believes he has drunk alcohol, whether in fact he has or not.[23] In other words, craving appears to be psychologically based rather than physiologically based.

A further test of this result was conducted in 1973.[24] Researchers asked alcoholic subjects, who were not aware their alcoholism was the reason they had been asked to volunteer for the experiment, to taste test various drinks. The subjects were divided into four groups. One group was asked to taste rate three different brands of vodka and was given vodka. The second group was asked to taste three different brands of vodka but was given tonic. The third group was asked to taste tonics but was given vodka. And the fourth group was asked to compare tonics and was given tonics. The tasters were allowed to drink, in private, as much as they liked for fifteen minutes in order to determine their preferences. A researcher, who was unaware of which group a subject belonged to, secretly observed each subject and recorded the number of sips he or she took. Data included how much of the beverage was consumed, sip rate, amount consumed per sip, and an estimate of the subject's ultimate blood alcohol level. A duplicate control experiment was conducted using subjects who were not alcoholics.

The alcoholics drank much more than the non-alcoholics in all groups. Significantly, all subjects who thought they were drinking alcohol drank more than those who thought they were drinking tonic. In other words, all drinkers, whether or not alcoholic, drank more according to their beliefs and expectations about what they were drinking, rather than according to the actual alcohol content of their drinks.

The above experiments (and numerous others) refute the idea that once an alcoholic takes a drink he will inevitably lose control over how much he consumes. This led one disease proponent to redefine what was meant by loss of control in this way: If an alcoholic has a drink, he *can never be sure* that he will be able to stop. Loss of control is thus seen as something intermittent and unpredictable.[25] This definition defies scientific testing, as it has been impossible to identify the conditions under which loss of control will occur and those under which it will not occur.

One thing is certain: It is easier to demonstrate an alcoholic's control in a laboratory setting than it is to observe it in his everyday environment. *Heavy Drinking* author Herbert Fingarette points out:

> ... the change in setting from home to hospital indeed radically affects alcoholics' self control and drinking patterns ... [It appears] it is the social setting, not any chemical effect of alcohol, that influences drinkers' abilities to exert control over their drinking.
>
> ... In these special [laboratory] settings, a drinker's self-control may also be reinforced by the *absence* of situations that prompt drinking at home, such as domestic or social frustrations, social enticements, or job anxieties. But clearly it is each drinker's perception of the pattern of positive and negative motivations, and not an uncontrollable abnormal chemical-physiological reaction, that decisively affects the choice to drink, to abstain, or to drink in moderation.[26]

A noted research team suggested another way of looking at it: "First drink, then drunk unless circumstances warrant stopping drinking."[27]

Physical Dependence

Consider the following example of physical dependence. Assume an individual drinks one shot of vodka every day. Over time, that individual will become tolerant to alcohol's effects — in other words, one shot will no longer produce the same pleasing high or sense of relaxation as it once did for her. She may then increase her daily intake to two shots.

The amount of time it takes a person's tolerance level to increase depends upon the person. Some people have naturally high tolerance levels; some have very low tolerance levels. Women in general have lower tolerance than men, and the greater a person's body weight, the higher his or her tolerance level is likely to be.

It may take a matter of months or even decades before the individual described above raises her daily alcohol intake to five or six shots a day, the amount when alcohol-related problems typically occur.[28] There is no timetable one can use to predict when, and by how much, an individual's tolerance level will rise.

So our increasingly tolerant drinker consumes more and more alcohol in search of a high that is a constantly moving target. Eventually, she becomes "physically dependent"; in other words, the cells in her body adapt to function normally in the presence of alcohol. She begins to experience signs of physical dependence whenever her blood alcohol levels fall. These typical "withdrawal" symptoms include shaking, nervousness, insomnia, appetite loss, nausea, excessive perspiration, and memory lapses. In fact, she may start to feel "hungover" even while she continues to drink if she's not drinking enough to maintain a certain blood alcohol concentration. Accompanying her withdrawal symptoms is the growing desire for a drink that will alleviate them.

So she has a drink to stave off withdrawal, perhaps at 7:00 in the morning. It calms her nerves and relaxes her. Rather than causing her to appear drunk or incapacitating her, the alcohol allows her to function normally. By maintaining a certain blood alcohol level for as long as possible, her withdrawal symptoms become that much more severe whenever her blood alcohol level drops. She no longer drinks to feel pleasure, as she may have in the past; now, she drinks just to keep from feeling awful. Although her total alcohol consumption could easily reach a fifth of vodka a day, a passing observer might not even be able to tell she has been drinking.

What happens when, in this severely dependent state, she does *not* drink to relieve withdrawal symptoms? After a couple of days of suffering from the usual, though severe, symptoms, alcohol will be completely out of her system. But her troubles don't end there. She may begin to experience seizures and then the delirium tremens (DTs), which, in the worst cases, can last a week or more. The DTs involve violent shaking, disorientation, and hallucinations. She will most likely be malnourished and dehydrated, and lab tests will probably detect some degree of liver damage. The DTs do not always require treatment (in the form of sedatives), but they can be fatal for those people who also have liver, pancreas, or kidney damage or who are suffering from other illnesses such as pneumonia.

If she has survived the DTs — alone or in a "detoxification unit" — and has not ingested any more alcohol, she is no longer physically dependent. In fact, only copious amounts of alcohol will reinstate the physical dependence. Why would she then, like most people in her place, go out and reinitiate the vicious cycle of tolerance and withdrawal?

Two researchers have put it this way: "'Detoxification,' or the removal of physical dependence, is now a relatively simple affair, and if that were all there was to solving a drinking problem, one could guarantee almost 100 percent success. The real difficulties, of course, only start after detoxification when the problem drinker returns to his or her home environment and the persons and situations associated with excessive drinking in the past. It is the prevention of relapse, or a return to harmful drinking, which represents the main task for treatment or the problem drinker's efforts at self-help."[29] The return to problem drinking after detox, therefore, seems to be a matter of *psychological* dependence.

Despite the effectiveness of detox (in the form of approximately two weeks of total abstinence), is physical dependence — also called addiction — a disease? Some experts have argued that physical dependence is a *learned behavior* that can be unlearned, rather than an illness like cancer. The simplest and most famous example of a learned physiological response is Pavlov's dogs.

In the early 1900s, Russian researcher Ivan Pavlov was studying the role of enzymes in digestion. To do so, he monitored the saliva production of dogs while they ate. He was surprised to discover that the dogs began to salivate as soon as they saw their empty food dish or an attendant approaching with their meat. He conducted experiments in which, for instance, he sent the attendant to the dogs with no food, eliminating the possibility that it was the smell of the meat that triggered the dogs' salivation. But the dogs still salivated. Their expectations triggered their physiological response. In further experiments, Pavlov showed that by ringing a bell whenever the dogs received meat, he could condition the dogs to salivate whenever they heard a bell ring, regardless of whether meat was present.

How does this relate to a dependent drinker? Let's say a heavy drinker stops by a bar after work every day for some drinks. His body has learned to expect an ounce of alcohol at 6:00. As alcohol has the effect of depressing the nervous system, his body counteracts that effect, in a process known as homeostasis, by activating or "exciting" its nervous system. By a quarter to six, the drinker's body knows what's coming, so it triggers its response by exciting the nerves — the drinker starts to feel nervous, shaky, and craves a drink, just as the dogs would salivate in anticipation of a meal.

Pavlov also discovered that if he sent the attendant to the dogs empty-handed often enough, the dogs would learn not to expect meat and therefore would not salivate. By the same logic, if you took the heavy drinker to his bar every day but didn't let him drink, his shaking and nervousness would eventually subside.

People may not be as easy to condition as dogs, but over time, heavy drinkers come to associate drinking with certain cues. The whistle that blows at the end of the workday can have as powerful an effect as Pavlov's bell. Cues could be a routine spat with a spouse at home, dinner with certain hard-drinking friends, common or mounting job frustrations, as well as the physical cues of shaking, sweating, and anxiety.

The authors of *Problem Drinking* argue that "The evidence suggests that relapses occur, not directly because of physical dependence, but because of social and psychological factors in the form of life events, lack of coping skills, and conditioned responses to alcohol-related cues — in short, because of aspects of problem drinking which have been learned. Thus, the abolition of physical dependence is a relatively unimportant part of the solution to a drinking problem and it is not helpful to exaggerate its importance by making it the cornerstone of a disease concept."[30]

A controversial figure in field of addiction research, Stanton Peele maintains, " ... addictive disorders *are known by the behaviors they describe* ... by claiming that alcoholics are alcoholics even if they haven't drunk for fifteen years, alcoholism is made to seem less tied to drinking behavior and more like cancer ... ."[31]

The result of thinking of addiction as if it were a disease like cancer is the exaggeration of the need for, and the use of, treatment. This is not to say that some people don't benefit greatly from treatment, whatever form it takes. However, we have come to accept that people with addictions are completely helpless and must become as dependent on treatment as they have been on their drugs. Evidence suggests that this notion is not true, and continuing to think of alcoholism in this way may actually have a negative effect on drinkers' recovery efforts.

Stanton Peele often uses cigarettes as an illustration of this point. He has informally surveyed scores of former addicts who were addicted to multiple substances and has asked them which substance was the most difficult to give up. Invariably "smoking cigarettes" was the top response. Yet very few of the numerous people who quit or reduce their smoking every day actually seek therapy or treatment to do so. Though it may contribute to illnesses such as heart disease and lung cancer, smoking is not considered a disease in the way that alcohol or drug addiction is. It thus *appears* that nicotine addiction is the easiest addiction to quit, even though addicts themselves tell us otherwise. Perhaps because we are given the impression that other substances, including alcohol, are so much more difficult to quit, we come to believe it — and come to believe in self-help groups and expensive treatment clinics more than in ourselves.

One could argue, of course, that it is a more urgent public health matter to help alcohol and drug abusers overcome their addictions than it is to help smokers overcome theirs. After all, smoking usually hurts only the smoker. Unlike other drug use, smoking does not compromise the addict's judgment and is unlikely to interfere with his job, with his marriage, with the raising of his children, or with his other social responsibilities.

Are the threats that problem drinkers pose to the public enough to justify labeling heavy drinking a disease and to propagate misleading information about the drinker's control, physical state, and recovery options? Good arguments exist on both sides of the debate, and Chapter 6 explores them. But first, let's examine what research authorities today regard as the true nature of problem drinking and its ramifications for recovery.

●

5 Bad Behavior

"Work is the curse of the drinking classes."
–Oscar Wilde

A S THE PREVIOUS chapter demonstrated, problem drinking does not conform to the elements of the classic disease theory. What, then, is problem drinking? Is it nonetheless a disease, only with a different definition?

Most scientists today believe that drinking (whether or not problematic) is a behavior that is learned, as are eating habits, responses to stress, and the way one expresses love or anger. Behavioral psychology has identified different ways in which people learn to develop their behaviors or habits.

First, drinking can be learned through the principles of classical and operant conditioning. When drinking leads to a pleasurable experience, for example, the drinker associates alcohol with that pleasure and becomes likely to drink again. Each subsequent positive drinking experience reinforces the connection between drinking and pleasure and further increases the likelihood of the person's drinking in the future. Even when the drinker starts to experience the negative consequences of drinking, from hangovers to withdrawal symptoms, he may continue drinking in the false hope that the original pleasure will resume.

Second, a drinker may model his behavior on that of an influential person. For instance, if a mother always drinks to cope with a stressful situation, her son may develop a similar tendency. If a teenager becomes more popular or outgoing when she drinks, her schoolmate may imitate that friend's drinking habits. If a successful boss throws back a couple of martinis at a business lunch, his underling may feel it is appropriate for him to do so as well.

A person's behavior can also be shaped by his expectations about what drinking will do for him. Such expectations can come from advertisements, movies, and observations of the effects of alcohol on others.

Finally, a person's culture can influence his drinking behavior. Social groups that are less tolerant of intoxicated behavior (such as Orthodox Jews) tend to have very low rates of alcoholism. On the other hand, one reason alcohol abuse is common among American teenagers may be *because* it is not socially acceptable inside that age group (in fact, it is illegal to sell alcohol to minors in the United States); drinking therefore becomes a way of expressing antisocial sentiments.

Instead of a disease, problem drinking can thus be seen as a self-destructive behavior, a bad habit, a compulsion, or an addiction. As briefly discussed in the previous chapter, addiction has been considered a disease, to the extent that physical dependence on the drug is present. As noted, however, removing physical dependence requires only a few days' abstinence — it's psychological dependence that's tough to shake. Does the persistent thought pattern of psychological dependence justify the label "disease"? Are other mental problems, such as anxiety, depression, and compulsive disorders, diseases? Nearly everyone is likely to experience anxiety or depression, for however limited a time, at some point in their lives, and many will overcome them without treatment, rather like colds.

As for addiction, Stanton Peele and Archie Brodsky, authors of *The Truth About Addiction and Recovery*, define it as:

> ... a habitual response and a source of grat-ification or security. It is a way of coping with internal feelings and external pressures that provides the addict with predictable gratifica-tions, but that has concomitant costs. Eventually these costs may outweigh the sub-jective benefits the addiction offers the indi-vidual. Nonetheless, people continue their addictions as long as they believe the addic-tions continue to do something for them ... .
>
> An addiction may involve *any* attachment or sensation that grows to such proportions that it damages a person's life. Addictions, no matter to what, follow certain common patterns ... .
>
> A person is vulnerable to addiction when that person feels a lack of satisfaction in life, an absence of intimacy or strong connections to other people, a lack of self-confidence or compelling interests, or a loss of hope.[1]

This conception leads to the conclusion that the best treatment for alcoholism would involve improving the addict's relationships, self-confidence, outlook on life, or helping him to develop new interests. Addiction thus seems to have more in common with depression than with, say, tuberculosis.

A dramatic example of this theory is the heroin addiction prevalent among American soldiers during the Vietnam War. Fighting a losing battle they may not have believed in, seeing their friends wounded and killed daily — it is no wonder many became heroin addicts, let alone depressed. After the war, researchers followed up on these men and learned that only half of the former addicts shot heroin after they returned to the United States, and only one-eighth of them became re-addicted. How could such a powerfully addictive drug be forsaken so easily? For one thing, the veterans suddenly had incentives not to shoot up: they had job prospects, the opportunity to see family and friends, and control over their lives back. They were removed from an environment of despair and death. The lesson: change the environment, show the addict he has opportunities for a better life, and the addiction can be broken. (Granted, changing the typical alcoholic's environment by relocating him halfway around the world is not a practical option, but the idea of changing the environment to some degree lies behind many therapies.)

More than one expert has pointed out the parallels between compulsive disorders (such as gambling, overeating, and shopping) and alcoholism. Peele, for instance, says, "gambling, like any other compulsive problem behavior, cannot be distinguished in etiology, treatment, or outcome from alcoholism or drug addiction."[2] Lying at the heart of these behavioral disorders may be a desire to escape a feeling of numbness or depression. In the *Natural History of Alcoholism Revisited*, George Vaillant offers the following explanation:

> Consider for example compulsive shoplifting, gambling, Russian roulette, and indecent exposure. None of these behaviors depends upon physical addiction. They are all under

very limited conscious control, they all have a life of their own, and all undoubtedly would disappear in a laboratory setting. All, however, involve a dramatic change of affective state.

We know that a change of mental state is more important when an individual is unhappy than when an individual is happy. The excitement of Russian roulette, of painful tattoos, of joining the Foreign Legion occurs among people who are demoralized and who possess impaired social networks. It is not that Russian roulette or exposing oneself or getting drunk necessarily makes one feel *good*, but what all three share is that they make one feel *different* ... .[3]

These conceptions of the nature of problem drinking have led to a number of treatments involving psychological and behavioral therapy, which are discussed in Chapter 7. A variety of treatment options, however, is not the only benefit that the modern conceptions of problem drinking have yielded. Now there is another option regarding the *goal* of treatment.

Command and Control

Treatments based on the classic disease concept of alcoholism, with its notions of irreversibility and loss of control, prescribe one goal: total abstinence. As the classic disease concept was eroded by reports of "normal" drinking among previously diagnosed alcoholics (see Chapter 4), researchers began to wonder whether "normal" or moderate drinking was a viable treatment goal for some alcoholics. Considering the uproar mere reports of normal drinking among alcoholics caused, it is no wonder that the so-called "controlled-drinking" studies attracted a considerable amount of controversy as well.

The first widely cited report of successful training for controlled drinking appeared in 1970. The researchers applied behavioral therapy techniques in treating thirty-one alcoholics, after which twenty-four managed to drink in a "controlled" manner for periods ranging from four months to a little over one year (the length of follow-up).[4] These results sparked an interest among other researchers who were eager to duplicate the study's outcome. In doing so, they sought to make up for the study's limitations, notably the lack of a control group.

One study, therefore, compared a controlled-drinking treatment program with one whose goal was abstinence.[5] Roughly one-third of each treatment group was abstinent for a year following treatment. Immediately following treatment, the members of both groups who were not abstinent had cut down to approximately half their pre-treatment alcohol consumption. Three months later, the drinkers in the group trained for abstinence were drinking 70 percent as much as they had before treatment, while the drinkers in the controlled-drinking group had further reduced their consumption to about 20 percent of their pre-treatment levels. Over six months' time, the drinkers in the controlled-drinking group continued to reduce their consumption by a greater amount than did those in the abstinence-oriented group.

The most controversial controlled-drinking study was reported in 1972, by researchers Mark and Linda Sobell. Their forty volunteer subjects were male inpatients at Patton State Hospital in California. The

Sobells divided them into four groups: (1) controlled-drinking-oriented behavioral treatment, (2) conventional abstinence-oriented treatment, (3) behavioral therapy aimed at abstinence, and (4) non-controlled-drinking therapy recommending, but not insisting upon, abstinence. The Sobells treated their controlled-drinking subjects with their own "Individualized Behavior Therapy" and evaluated their subjects' outcomes with the following measures:

- Drunk days: consumption of greater than six ounces of 86-proof liquor or its equivalent in alcohol content.
- Controlled-drinking days: consumption of six ounces or less of 86-proof liquor or its equivalent in alcohol content.
- Abstinent days: no consumption of any type of alcohol.
- Incarcerated days/jail: days spent in jail for alcohol-related arrests.
- Incarcerated days/hospital: days spent in a hospital for alcohol-related health problems, usually detoxification.
- Other measures of success: general adjustment, vocational status, occupational status, residential status and stability index, valid driver's license status, marital status, use of therapeutic supports, possession of research program "do's and do not's card," physical health evaluation.[6]

At the end of their study, the Sobells concluded that "subjects who received the program of Individualized Behavior Therapy (IBT) with a treatment goal of controlled drinking ... functioned significantly better throughout the two-year follow-up period than did their respective control subjects ... who received conventional abstinence-oriented treatment."[7] They also noted that "only subjects treated by IBT with a goal of controlled drinking successfully engaged in a substantial amount of limited, non-problem drinking during the two years of follow-up, and those subjects also had more abstinent days than subjects in any other group."[8]

It wasn't long before critics began to attack the integrity of the Sobells' research. Mary Pendery, the director of an alcohol-treatment center in Southern California, received funding to do an extensive follow-up investigation of the Sobell's study. Ten years after the Sobell study, her findings were published in the respected journal *Science*.[9] She and her co-authors all but accused the Sobells of fraud. Soon after, in March 1983, *60 Minutes* aired a segment on the Sobell study, interviewing Mary Pendery, but not the Sobells. The report, as could be expected, was further damaging to the Sobells' reputation. In response to media attacks, the Sobells asked the Addiction Research Foundation in Toronto to set up an independent committee to investigate the charges against them. The committee's findings became known as the Dickens Report.[10]

Among its many criticisms, the Dickens Report faulted Pendery's study for citing data out of context. Pendery reported, for instance, that four of the twenty subjects who received controlled-drinking training had died as the result of alcohol-related problems. The Dickens Report revealed, however, that Pendery had failed to point out that the deaths occurred between six and eleven years after treatment, and that *more* — in fact, six — of the twenty subjects in the abstinence-oriented control group had died during the same period. Furthermore, the Dickens Report found accusations that the Sobells had suppressed certain findings to be completely without merit. In conclusion, the Dickens

Report found no reasonable cause to doubt the scientific or personal integrity of the Sobells. A further Congressional investigation into the matter supported this conclusion.[11]

During the whole affair, the media had stressed the accusations, not the vindications, so the general public was left with the impressions it got from television news programs and newspaper articles: that controlled-drinking treatment was a sham.

Another controlled-drinking study involved randomly dividing seventy problem drinkers, who were each drinking roughly seventy ounces of alcohol per week, into an abstinence group and a controlled-drinking group (whose members were asked to abstain for the first four sessions of treatment). During the first three weeks, the members of the abstinence group drank much more than the controlled-drinking group and significantly more of the controlled-drinking group actually abstained. A year later, no significant difference existed between the groups, but the abstinence group had sought help more frequently than had the controlled drinkers.[12]

A study of male veterans divided participants into two groups: one receiving abstinence-oriented treatment and the other receiving controlled-drinking treatment. After six months, the severely dependent members of the controlled-drinking group experienced more days of heavy drinking than did those in the abstinence group; however, after one year, the differences disappeared, and at six years there were no significant differences between the two groups.[13]

A Step on the Road to Abstinence

One might think that controlled-drinking treatment would appeal to every alcoholic, but this is not the case. In one study of sixty-three alcohol-dependent men given the choice in treatment goals between abstinence and controlled drinking, roughly 70 percent chose abstinence.[14] Indeed, controlled-drinking studies have shown that most people who moderate their drinking eventually abstain. According to one researcher, "Our long-term follow-up research with clients treated with a moderation goal found that more wound up abstaining than moderating their drinking without problems."[15]

Other researchers have reached similar conclusions. In one study, 75 percent of participants who reported previous drinking problems recovered without formal treatment (i.e., eliminated all problems resulting from overdrinking), and 50 percent achieved stable, moderate drinking.[16] University of Washington Professor G. Alan Marlatt concludes, "Contrary to the progressive disease model, these findings indicate that a majority of individuals with drinking problems recover on their own ... . Even when they are trained in controlled drinking, many alcohol-dependent individuals choose abstinence. Over time, rates of abstinence (as compared to controlled drinking) tend to increase."[17]

Candidates for Controlled Drinking

Who responds best to controlled-drinking therapy? In general, people under 40 who have suffered less severe dependence-related problems, people with stable marital or family relationships, people with stable employment, and women.

Younger people and those whose problems are not that severe are notoriously difficult to attract into conventional treatment and to persuade to adopt a goal of abstinence. A four-year follow-up of the Rand Report (see p. 59) showed that young, unmarried men with a low level of dependence were ten times more likely to relapse if they had adopted abstinence as a goal than if they had become moderate, non-problem drinkers eighteen months after treatment.[18] Offering young drinkers the option of controlled-drinking counseling may therefore draw them into treatment sooner and thus prevent them from developing worse drinking problems down the line.

Even in cases in which abstinence is clearly the most pragmatic treatment goal (for example, for a 55-year-old male who has been in and out of detox wards for thirty-five years), offering the option of moderation may at least bring the person into treatment he might otherwise shun. Once the person is in treatment, a failed attempt at controlled drinking may prove the case for abstinence more persuasively than would a confrontational therapist citing disease-theory dogma for hours on end. As Dr. Marlatt puts it, "From a public health perspective, it makes sense to offer moderation-oriented programs to alcohol abusers and mildly dependent individuals as a means of increasing client recruitment and retention. Individuals who do not benefit from these programs can be 'stepped up' to more intensive abstinence-oriented services."[19]

Another expert, Dr. Reid K. Hester, agrees that the less dependent "problem drinker population has been largely ignored, or at least underserved. To offer only one alternative — total abstention — is to turn away a large population in need of services."[20]

Aside from age, gender, and marital and employment

status, another predictor of success with controlled drinking is the person's belief about her chances for success. If she has come to believe that abstinence is the only course, then persuading her otherwise will be counterproductive. The authors of *The Miracle Method* point out, "What seems to matter is whether or not the person believes he or she can control his or her drinking."[21]

Furthermore, another expert contends that there is enough proof that "people's response to treatment depends more on how they think about themselves than on the severity of their actual symptoms. For example, people who believe they can drink moderately are more likely to actually succeed at controlling their drinking, contrary to AA's denial theory ... . Indeed, we're more likely to adhere to treatment goals that we participate in setting."[22]

In addition to the overall benefits of attracting more problem drinkers into treatment, controlled-drinking therapies also offer other benefits over abstinence-only therapies. When the Sobells interviewed their controlled-drinking subjects about what they believed to be the benefits of their treatment, they responded with the following comments: "[Controlled drinking] allows a person to retain his dignity. One can escape the effects of labeling. One learns to deal with problems and it takes the fear away from the bottle."[23] Another expert points out that controlled drinking gives problem drinkers "the opportunity to develop the self-image of 'regular person,' a person with a normal range of problems."[24]

Therapists use various techniques to assess whether a person is a good candidate for controlled drinking. The following "decision tree" is an example of how therapists help clients choose treatment goals.

A tentative decision tree for those male clients wishing to control their drinking

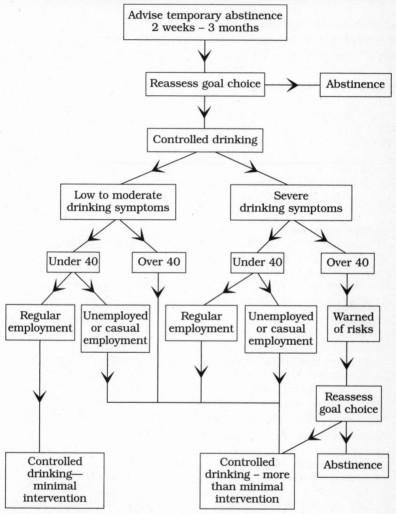

Reprinted with permission from *Controlled Drinking*, by Nick Heather and Ian Robertson (Methuen, 1981).

Controlled drinking, like abstinence, can be the goal of a number of therapies based on behavioral psychology. While specific treatment approaches are discussed in Chapter 7, the following table gives some idea of the treatment options available.

Some examples of the applications of psychological processes to alcoholic behavior

Psychological process
Examples of its application
to alcoholic behavior

Examples of psychological
treatments following from
this analysis

Classical conditioning
(1) Reduction of withdrawal symptoms
by further drinking ("relief drinking").
(2) Warmth, companionship, and
pleasant surroundings present while
drinking alcohol but absent when
not drinking.
(3) Stomach pain following alcohol
ingestion resulting in a reduction
in drinking.

Electrical aversion,
chemical aversion,
cue exposure

Skilled behavior
(1) Inability to drink slowly.
(2) Inability to refuse drinks.
(3) Inability to occupy leisure
time enjoyably other than by drinking.

Regulated drinking
practice. BAC
discrimination training,
social skills training.

Self-control
(1) Absence of accurate self-
monitoring of alcohol intake.
(2) Failure to recognize situations
where heavy drinking is likely.
(3) Absence of a set of "working
rules" governing drinking behavior.
(4) Absence of system of "self-rewards"
for non-drinking and moderate drinking.

Self-management
training, including:
self-monitoring,
stimulus control, rule
setting, self-reward,
self-punishment

Cognitive learning
(1) Disorganized and unconstructive
cognitive responses to stress in
the form of such self-statements
as "I give up" or "My life is a mess."
(2) Expectation of loss of control
following small intake of alcohol.
(3) Attribution of a slip following
a decision to abstain to personal
weakness.
(4) Belief that a large intake of
alcohol produces beneficial
personality changes.

Problem-solving skills
training, self-
instructional training,
rational emotive therapy,
cognitive therapy, anxiety
management

Reprinted with permission from *Controlled Drinking*,
by Nick Heather and Ian Robertson (Methuen, 1981).

The Reasons for Resistance

Controlled-drinking therapies are part of the standard treatment menu at clinics in Canada, the U.K., and other European countries, but American treatment centers are notoriously resistant to offering controlled-drinking counseling. Considering all the reports of normal drinking among formerly diagnosed alcoholics, as well as all the evidence supplied by controlled-drinking studies since 1970, why do the people who work in twenty-eight-day treatment clinics still deny that moderate drinking can be a stable treatment outcome for many problem drinkers?

One reason is that a great number of them have "been through the system." They themselves had drinking problems and recovered through the twelve-step method. They are therefore more likely to believe that what worked for them can work for everyone.

Another reason is that they do not witness moderate drinking outcomes among the clients they have treated. Clients who successfully return to moderate drinking patterns after being treated with a goal of abstinence have no reason to keep in contact with their therapists, especially if those therapists constantly decry their moderation goals. Harvard researcher George Vaillant put it this way: "Confronted by thousands of clients who are unable to control their drinking, clinicians are understandably unimpressed. But, of course, once an alcoholic patient returns to social drinking, the clinician loses track. Unlike researchers, clinicians maintain contact only with problem drinkers."[25]

A more financial motive lies behind the following explanation made by British observers: "Because those attending these clinics are often funded either by private or government insurance schemes, there is a powerful incentive among owners of the clinics to propagate the view that alcoholism is a disease; if it is not, then funders may be less likely to support long in-patient treatment programmes."[26]

Those clinicians who do acknowledge that moderation is a possible outcome often see it as a *temporary* outcome. They typically believe that controlled drinking inevitably gives way to uncontrolled drinking, no matter how long the controlled-drinking behavior has been maintained. They often fail to recognize that abstinence is at least as unstable an outcome as moderation.

To sum up, controlled-drinking treatment can

- help draw into treatment people who otherwise would not bother to seek it;
- prevent early-stage problem drinkers from developing more serious problems;
- help drinkers retain "normal" self-images; and
- persuade more severely dependent drinkers of their need for abstinence.

Like abstinence-oriented treatment, controlled drinking will not work for everyone. One AA catchphrase applies equally well to people who pursue controlled-drinking goals: "Easy does it." Or, as the authors of *Problem Drinking* warn:

> ... when one speaks of normal drinking in alcoholics, it is often assumed that one is describing an "easy option" compared with abstinence; problem drinkers may believe that a return to normal drinking is something they can accomplish without much effort or pain. The truth is the very opposite. For those with a severe level of dependence and a long history of heavy drinking, a harm-free pattern of use is extraordinarily difficult to achieve, and this

is why such persons should typically be advised to abstain. *A decision to aim for controlled drinking in someone with a serious and long-standing problem should only be made after seeking competent professional advice.*[27]

•

The Films of Wine and Four Roses

Hollywood has had considerable influence on increasing public awareness of tragic illnesses and disabilities (think AIDS and *Philadelphia*, cerebral palsy and *My Left Foot*, deafness and *Children of a Lesser God*). Indeed, the film industry has taken a starring role in shaping public opinion about alcoholism as well.[29]

The Lost Weekend, for instance, starring Ray Milland and Jane Wyman and directed by Billy Wilder, had an enormous impact on public perceptions of problem drinking by presenting the AA version of an alcoholic's decline and fall. Winning the Best Picture Oscar of 1945, it forcefully portrayed alcoholism as a disease: The drinker's girlfriend pleads for sympathy, "He's a sick person!" And to prove it, he winds up in a horrific detox ward inhabited by hallucinating drunks in the throes of the DTs. Ray Milland's character describes his battle with the bottle as though he were reading directly from the Big Book of AA. His dialogue strains credibility, as there are probably few alcoholics who possess so much insight into their problems. At the end of the movie, his character recovers with a determination to write a novel of his experiences, mirroring AA's twelfth step to "carry this message to alcoholics."

A more realistic picture of alcoholism came in the 1962 film *The Days of Wine and Roses*, starring Academy Award nominees Jack Lemmon and Lee Remick and directed by Blake Edwards. A couple living the high life in San Francisco finds their relationship and careers washed away by booze. One of them finds salvation through AA and clings to it; the other is cast adrift. Despite their enormous love for one another, the husband comes to value his sobriety more than his relationship with his wife — a painful realization for both of them.

In perhaps the most riveting performance of an alcoholic, Nicolas Cage won the 1995 Best Actor award for his role in *Leaving Las Vegas*, also starring Elisabeth Shue and directed by Mike Figgis. Set in the capital of compulsive behavior, Cage's character is contrasted with Shue's, a jaded prostitute. Both unwilling to change their ways, the couple form a unique bond built on their respect for each other's lifestyles. Determined to drink himself to death, Cage's character eventually succeeds, making all the unpleasant stops along the way.

Overlooked by the Academy, but making

many critics' Top Ten lists in 1988, *Barfly* depicted another boozehound's unquenchable thirst. Based on writer Charles Bukowski's novel, the film is a detailed character study whose protagonist waxes rhapsodic about his relationship with alcohol:

> This thing upon me like a flower and a feast ... This thing upon me crawling like a snake. It's not death, but dying will solve its power ... . And as my hands drop a last desperate pen in some cheap room, they will find me there and never know my name, my meaning, nor the treasure of my escape.

Not that all boozers are treated so bleakly: From Nick and Nora, the sleuthing swells of the *Thin Man* films, to the suave sophistication of James Bond's shaken-not-stirred martini, to the one-liners slurred through the lips of sloshed playboy Arthur, Hollywood films have also depicted drink as an accoutrement to a swinging, successful life.

•

6 Attitude Adjustment

*"What biomedicine finds hard to recognize or to accept
is that different observers — patient, spouse, doctor,
pastor, insurance provider, hospital administrator,
epidemiologist, to name a few — examining the same
illness from their separate perspectives will observe
different aspects of its truth."*
–David B. Morris, *Illness and Culture
in the Postmodern Age*

LET'S SUPPOSE WE accept the current scientific thinking and believe problem drinking to be a learned behavior that is reversible. Let's further assume that therapists trained in behavioral psychology can help problem drinkers reestablish control over their drinking habits and improve their overall lives. Would it nonetheless still be helpful for the public as well as the problem drinker to think of alcoholism as a disease?

The word "disease" carries two important connotations. For one, it connotes a condition over which the afflicted have no control and for which they have no responsibility. A disease is thought of as something that happens *to* a person. Second, its treatment is seen as something medical that is administered to a patient by a physician.

Disease proponents argue that attributing the drinker's problems to a disease outside her control frees her from the guilt and stigma of moral weakness. It clears her conscience enough to admit the problem and not be ashamed to seek help.

But doesn't the disease perspective merely swap one stigma — that of moral failing — for another — that of being diseased? By assigning responsibility for the problem to something outside the person, it tells him, in effect, that he is powerless and therefore helpless. The person learns to think of himself as a victim. As he is told he can never fully recover, his victim status is now permanent. He begins to define himself by his problem.

Stanton Peele, one of the most outspoken critics of conventional addiction treatment, has observed that recovering alcoholics often seem "burdened with their alcoholic or addicted self-image to a degree that hinders their functioning" and that they are able to "use their addicted identity to explain all their previous problems without actually doing anything concrete to improve their performance."[1] He accuses traditional treatment of ignoring "the rest of the person's problems in favor of blaming them all on the addiction"[2] and limiting clients' "human contacts primarily to other recovering alcoholics who only reinforce their preoccupation with drinking";[3] in effect, trapping them "in a world inhabited by fellow disease sufferers" until they "feel comfortable only with others in exactly the same plight."[4]

To reject the disease label is not to deny that problem drinkers deserve help and compassion. The authors of *Problem Drinking* argue, " ... a disease concept of alcoholism classifies *people*, whereas a more useful perspective invites a classification of *behaviour*. When we think of problem drinking, we should think immediately of the particular behaviour which causes drinking to be recognized as a problem, rather than of a person who is thereby separated from the rest of mankind."[5]

Wouldn't it, therefore, be more productive for the drinker to think he has a personality weakness he can overcome, rather than a lifelong disease he can never shake? Might not the shame of a moral failure be put to good use? Some people have wondered, Why shouldn't alcoholics feel ashamed of their behavior? Wouldn't a greater sense of shame have prevented the behavior in the first place?

Perhaps not as long as "twelve-stepping" dominates treatment and its social appeal builds. The shame of drinking heavily almost seems worth the price of the pride one can take in being "in recovery." There was a time when celebrities would hide their addictions from the public; now it seems as though admitting you've been through rehab is a badge of honor and, in fact, a significant publicity "op." British researchers observing America's predilection for twelve-step solutions have commented on how recovery through twelve-step programs confers social "cachet":

> The application of AA dogmas to behaviours which could scarcely be termed "diseases" — shopping, for instance — with all the paraphernalia about recognizing these as illnesses over which one has no control, has a faintly ludicrous quality. Their acceptance by many Americans testifies to the fact that what we are witnessing here is a socio-religious phenomenon requiring of followers the confession and repentance through which they receive status and acceptance.
>
> Hence the attempt to explain alcohol prob-

lems, as well as other drug problems, in non-disease terms not only steps on commercial toes by threatening the theoretical basis for disease-based treatment programmes, it also threatens an entire social movement by asserting that there are other means of breaking habits than by confession and repentance.[6]

Conventional treatment for alcoholism gains the public's compassion for the alcoholic by publicizing the disease perspective. But this treatment is not medically based — it is actually morally based. Indeed, by requiring the drinker to submit herself to a Higher Power, AA takes an essentially moral approach to solving the alcoholic's problem. Jack Trimpey, co-founder of Rational Recovery and author of *The Small Book*, writes, "The program simply assumes that by becoming morally good, people will stay sober ... alcoholism is viewed very clearly as a moral failure, as separation from God, as a spiritual deficit to be remedied by a religious conversion."[7]

What good is thinking of alcoholism as a disease when the drinker is told that the only available treatment is based on the idea that alcoholism is a moral failing? What good is it to tell someone they are sick and powerless, but then send them to a self-help group, rather than to a doctor, for treatment? Philosopher Herbert Fingarette pointed out this paradox in his book *Heavy Drinking*: "If the alcoholic's ailment is a disease that causes an inability to abstain from drinking, how can a program insist on voluntary abstention as a condition for treatment? (And if alcoholics who enter these programs do voluntarily abstain — as in fact they generally do — then of what value is the [disease] notion of loss of control?)"[8]

From the perspective of the alcoholism-as-behav-ioral-disorder model, a moral approach may make sense, to a point. As Douglas Cameron, author of *Liberating Solutions to Alcohol Problems*, has argued, "Those of us who choose to engage repetitively in pleas-urable but potentially damaging activities (car driving, drinking, hang gliding, sex) are quite rightly the subject of moral scrutiny. Those behaviours are a matter of morality. Attempting to cloak ourselves in a 'mantle of sickness' does not remove the moral dimension."[9]

Alternative treatments address the moral issues of drinking not by preaching to the patient, but by attempting to redirect the person's values. They do this by helping the drinker to discover reasons to value his life, his health, his relationships, etc. more than he val-ues the effects of alcohol.

Although the word "disease" implies a medical condi-tion requiring the services of a medical doctor, when AA and traditional therapies succeed, they do so largely without medical supervision. As previously discussed, a fair number of problem drinkers recover on their own, without any professional intervention at all. With the exception of a few drug therapies (discussed in Chapter 7), there is rarely anything medical about alcoholism treatment.

Of course, there may be nothing medical about the treatment for, say, heart disease when it involves only changes in diet and exercise. Alternatively, there are conditions requiring medical attention that are not con-sidered diseases, such as burns and broken bones. As George Vaillant, author of *The Natural History of Alcoholism* argues, " ... however dexterously alcoholism may be shoehorned into a medical model, both its eti-ology and its treatment are largely social. Indeed, in modern medicine there may be no other instance of sociology's contributing so much to our understanding of a so-called disease."[10] Nonetheless, Dr. Vaillant believes that considering alcoholism a disease has important advantages: " ... calling alcoholism a disease, rather than a behavior disorder, is a useful device both to persuade the alcoholic to admit his alcoholism and to provide a ticket for admission into the health care system."[11]

So far, however, the healthcare system has not done much to help alcoholics. A recent nationwide survey of 648 physicians by the National Center on Addiction and Substance Abuse at Columbia University found that when presented with a patient showing early signs of alcoholism, 94 percent of primary care physicians failed to diagnose alcohol abuse. Furthermore, while 86 percent of doctors felt treatment for high blood pressure is very effective, only 4 percent believed treatment for alcoholism is effective. "A ticket for admission," therefore, may simply take the patient for a ride if the doctor can't diagnose the problem or provide an adequate treatment.

Dr. Vaillant argues, however, that the main benefit of physician involvement is not necessarily effective treatment, but peace of mind for the patient:

> The sanctioned healer should have status and power and be equipped with an unambiguous conceptual model of the problem, which he is willing to explain to the patient. (Within the medical model of alcoholism, this is the strategy behind Jellinek's disease concept.) Enhancement of the patient's self-esteem and reduction of his anxiety are the inevitable consequences ... . The point is that

if one cannot cure an illness, one wants to make the patient less afraid and overwhelmed by it.[12]

The reality appears to be that general practitioners themselves are so overwhelmed by it that they choose not to discuss it with their patients at all.

In fact, doctors may be encouraged by insurers not to waste their time diagnosing alcoholics. Patients may look to medicine to solve all their problems, but our insurance industry looks elsewhere. It aims to contain costs and solve as many health problems with as little medical intervention as possible. Economics are now determining what is and isn't a medical problem, or, as David Morris, author of *Illness and Culture in the Postmodern Age*, points out, "In the United States today, an illness does not count as an illness unless an HMO will certify it. So much for biology alone."[13]

The rising cost of healthcare, among other things, has helped force us to see how we can better prevent illnesses from occurring in the first place. Just as we have become more suspicious of our surroundings in an effort to discover and reduce environmental causes of illnesses, we have become more comfortable analyzing how our behavior makes us susceptible to illnesses and more willing to change our habits accordingly. Even Dr. Vaillant admits,

> Good health will often be more dependent upon altering habits than upon visiting doctors. Indeed, the disease paradigm has probably slowed advances in management of diabetes, hypertension, and coronary heart disease. Had these disorders, like alcoholism, been reclassified as disorders of human

behavior, greater emphasis would have been placed sooner on paramount issues of appropriate health-care delivery mechanisms, compliance monitoring, alteration of lifestyles, and the patient's motivation. Effective treatment will always gain much from undoing the simplistic thinking of the medical model.[14]

Medical science can offer only a fraction of help in explaining and treating alcoholism, yet it is often the first place the public and the government turn to for new solutions. With this public mandate, researchers can become so absorbed by their own line of inquiry that they fail to see the bigger picture. Genetic research, as discussed in Chapter 3, falls prey to this trap. Scientists can become so enamored with the potential of genetic research that they fail to recognize that other factors — social and environmental — may contribute more to the development of an illness. As a result, they (as well as the general public) also fail to see how treatments that are socially or environmentally based may be more desirable and cost-effective than possible genetic treatments. Classifying alcoholism as primarily a medical problem thus closes the door to public funding of more effective and widely accessible solutions. Dr. Vaillant illustrates this point dramatically:

> When investigators focus only upon one class of data in a multifactorial problem, the results can range from misleading to preposterous. I have listened to Nobel Laureates and famous biochemists discuss the dream that the morbidity of alcoholism would be cured if one could predict the hepatic alcohol transam-

inase, and thereby prevent cirrhosis. Apparently, traffic fatalities, battered wives, and the despair of a life spent on Skid Row escaped their attention.[15]

The danger of constantly telling people that they have no control is that eventually they may come to believe it. They are therefore likely to lose both hope and the spirit to fight their destructive urges. They become prone to depression.

On the other hand, when you tell someone that, with time and effort, he *can* change his habits, make improvements to troublesome aspects of his life, and reverse the course of his drinking problems, he will probably be more willing to give treatment a try and recognize the signs of his progress. By showing him he has choices for treatment, you provide more hope and give him back a sense of control simply by allowing him to choose.

Ideally, treatment centers could offer all of the approaches described in the next chapter and let the client decide how best to view his problem. Arguing over the disease label may merely waste time. As the Sobells noted in *Behavioral Treatment of Alcohol Problems*, " ... allegiance to theoretical positions does little to encourage progress in the scientific study of alcohol problems. In fact, it can discourage innovative research developments. Notions presented by Jellinek as hypotheses in need of scientific test have been treated by others as though they were demonstrated facts and have been offered as evidence supporting popular beliefs."[16] Finishing this thought, *Heavy Drinking* author Herbert Fingarette concluded, "But to invoke the mantle of science in this way, no matter how worthy the social goals, ultimately is a disservice, for it prevents the public from engaging in a free and open debate of truly controversial issues that involve millions of persons and billions of dollars."[17]

Despite the best PR efforts of disease proponents, Americans are still conflicted about the nature of problem drinking. Although we might admit to thinking of alcoholism as a disease, we still make moral judgments about people who have drinking problems. Why, for instance, might we look at one person and say, "That slob should be ashamed of himself!" and then say of another, "This poor guy is sick and needs help!"? In the first instance, we see the person's drunkenness as a character weakness; in the second, we see a victim of a disease that's beyond his control. Certain prejudices — particularly how we respond to a person when he's sober — undoubtedly affect our view of alcoholism in individual cases. If we think a person is a jerk when he's sober, for example, we're likely to think he's an even bigger jerk when he's drunk — thus attributing his drunken state to personality flaws. If we like and respect the person when he's sober, however, we might look more compassionately at his drinking problem. These unconscious responses to individuals are not likely to change overnight.

Still, for wider, social purposes, deciding whether to view problem drinking as a disease may come down to asking ourselves, Do we really need another disease? Aren't we already burdened with enough fears of truly incurable diseases like cancer, AIDS, and Ebola? Problem drinking represents the extreme state of a normal, typically healthy activity — just as eating too much or too little, exercising too much or too little, and worrying too much or too little fall on either ends of a spectrum of necessary, unavoidable activity. It is by a process of learning and growing that we decide where along that spectrum an activity best fulfills our personal needs. Deciding is a daily undertaking, a lifelong endeavor, and sometimes involves seeking outside advice. Decisions change along with the circumstances of environment and aging. Stanton Peele warns, "By elevating the unhealthy side of normal functioning to the status of disease state, therapists and others who claim the mantle of science now *guarantee* the preeminence, pervasiveness, and persistence of sickness in everyday life."[18] He further laments:

> Because internal (psychological) and external (environmental) factors are given short shrift in disease views, we lose hope of changing our worlds. In the diseased world, striving for personal and social goals becomes secondary to counteracting unchangeable, inbred maladies. Disease views, in this way, attack the human and social values that make our lives worth living. The whole focus of our society becomes more pessimistic and self-preoccupied ... .[19]

There is ample evidence that, with sufficient motivation, we can break free of our addictions. See it as hard work, certainly. But to see it as next to impossible serves little purpose.

•

The Supreme Court v. The Disease Theory

Despite the so-called War on Drugs, one might get the impression that the courts are sympathetic to the plight of substance abusers. One need only recall the infamous "Twinkie defense" that resulted in the acquittal of a sugar-addled man who had murdered two San Francisco politicians. First-time offenders may be ordered into rehab rather than jail, depending on the nature of their crime. Nevertheless, addicts and abusers of all substances, including alcohol, must face the legal consequences of their behavior. Whatever benefits an alcoholic may gain by believing she is not responsible for her behavior, avoiding legal responsibility for any crimes she commits while under the influence is not one of them.

While the public may have accepted the disease theory of alcoholism, the U.S. Supreme Court has not. Below is an abridged transcript of the majority opinion of the Court in the 1968 case of *Powell v. Texas*.[20] The case involved the alcoholic defendant Leroy Powell's public intoxication, an offense in the Texas county from which the appeal originated. Justice Thurgood Marshall wrote the majority opinion, in which Chief Justice Warren, Justice Black, and Justice Harlan joined, and which Justice White affirmed (Justice Fortas wrote the dissent, with which Justices Douglas, Brennan, and Stewart joined).

In late December, 1966, appellant was arrested and charged with being found in a state of intoxication in a public place, in violation of Texas Penal Code, Art. 477(1952) ... .

... The trial judge in the county court, sitting without a jury, made certain findings of fact ... but ruled as a matter of law that chronic alcoholism was not a defense to the charge. He found appellant guilty, and fined him $50. There being no further right to appeal within the Texas judicial system, appellant appealed to this Court; we noted probable jurisdiction. 389 U.S. 810 (1967) ... .

... The principal testimony was that of Dr. David Wade, a Fellow of the American Medical Association, duly certificated in psychiatry ... . Dr. Wade sketched the outlines of the "disease" concept of alcoholism; noted that there is no generally accepted definition of "alcoholism"; alluded to the ongoing debate within the medical profession over whether alcohol is actually physically "addicting" or merely psychologically "habituating," and concluded that, in either case a "chronic alcoholic" is an "involuntary drinker," who is "powerless not to drink," and who "loses his self control over his drinking." He testified that he had examined appellant, and that appellant is a "chronic alcoholic," who by the time he has reached [the state of intoxication] ... , is not able to control his behavior, and [who] ... has reached this point because he has an uncontrollable compulsion to drink.

Dr. Wade also responded in the negative to the question whether appellant has "the willpower to resist the constant excessive consumption of alcohol." He added that, in his opinion, jailing appellant without medical attention would operate neither to rehabilitate him nor to lessen his desire for alcohol.

On cross-examination, Dr. Wade admitted that, when appellant was sober, he knew the difference between right and wrong, and he responded affirmatively to the question whether appellant's act of taking the first drink in any given instance when he was sober was a "voluntary exercise of his will." ... Appellant testified concerning the history of his drinking problem. He reviewed his many arrests for drunkenness; testified that he was unable to stop drinking; stated that, when he was intoxicated, he had no control over his actions and could not remember them later, but that he did not become violent, and admitted that he did not remember his arrest on the occasion for which he was being tried. On cross-examination, appellant admitted that he had had one drink on the morning of the trial, and had been able to discontinue drinking. In relevant part, the cross-examination went as follows:

Q. You took that one at eight o'clock because you wanted to drink?

A. Yes, sir.

Q. And you knew that, if you drank it, you could keep on drinking and get drunk?

A. Well, I was supposed to be here on trial, and I didn't take but that one drink.

Q. You knew you had to be here this afternoon, but, this morning, you took one drink and then you knew that you couldn't afford to drink any more and come to court; is that right?

A. Yes, sir, that's right.

Q. So you exercised your willpower and kept from drinking anything today except that one drink?

A. Yes, sir, that's right.

Q. Because you knew what you would do if you kept drinking, that you would finally pass out or be picked up?

A. Yes, sir.

Q. And you didn't want that to happen to you today?

A. No, sir.

Q. Not today?

A. No, sir.

Q. So you only had one drink today?

A. Yes, sir.

On redirect examination, appellant's lawyer elicited the following:

Q. Leroy, isn't the real reason why you just had one drink today because you just had enough money to buy one drink?

A. Well, that was just give to me.

Q. In other words, you didn't have any money with which you could buy any drinks yourself?

A. No, sir, that was give to me.

Q. And that's really what controlled the amount you drank this morning, isn't it?

A. Yes, sir.

Q. Leroy, when you start drinking, do you have any control over how many drinks you can take?

A. No, sir.

Evidence in the case then closed. The State made no effort to obtain expert psychiatric testimony of its own, or even to explore with appellant's witness the question of appellant's power to control the frequency, timing, and location of his drinking bouts, or the substantial disagreement within the medical profession concerning the nature of the disease, the efficacy of treatment and the prerequisites for effective treatment. It did nothing to examine or illuminate what Dr. Wade might have meant by his reference to a "compulsion" which was "not completely overpowering," but which was "an exceedingly strong influence," or to inquire into the question of the proper role of such a "compulsion" in constitutional adjudication. Instead, the State contented itself with a brief argument that appellant had no defense to the charge because he "is legally sane and knows the difference between right and wrong."

Following this abbreviated exposition of the problem before it, the trial court indicated its intention to disallow appellant's claimed defense of "chronic alcoholism." Thereupon, defense counsel submitted, and the trial court entered, the following "findings of fact":

(1) That chronic alcoholism is a disease which destroys the afflicted person's willpower to resist the con-

stant, excessive consumption of alcohol.

(2) That a chronic alcoholic does not appear in public by his own volition, but under a compulsion symptomatic of the disease of chronic alcoholism.

(3) That Leroy Powell, defendant herein, is a chronic alcoholic who is afflicted with the disease of chronic alcoholism.

Whatever else may be said of them, those are not "findings of fact" in any recognizable, traditional sense in which that term has been used in a court of law ... . Nonetheless, the dissent would have us adopt these "findings" without critical examination; it would use them as the basis for a constitutional holding that a person may not be punished if the condition essential to constitute the defined crime is part of the pattern of his disease and is occasioned by a compulsion symptomatic of the disease.

The difficulty with that position, as we shall show, is that it goes much too far on the basis of too little knowledge. In the first place, the record in this case is utterly inadequate to permit the sort of informed and responsible adjudication which alone can support the announcement of an important and wide-ranging new constitutional principle. We know very little about the circumstances surrounding the drinking bout which resulted in this conviction, or about Leroy Powell's drinking problem, or indeed about alcoholism itself ... .

Furthermore, the inescapable fact is that there is no agreement among members of the medical profession about what it means to say that "alcoholism" is a "disease." One of the principal works in this field states that the major difficulty in articulating a "disease concept of alcoholism" is that "alcoholism has too many definitions, and disease has practically none." [E. Jellinek, *The Disease Concept of Alcoholism*, p. 11 (1960).] This same author concludes that *"a disease is what the medical profession recognizes as such."* [*Id.* at 12; emphasis in original.] In other words, there is widespread agreement today that "alcoholism" is a "disease," for the simple reason that the medical profession has concluded that it should attempt to treat those who have drinking problems. There, the agreement stops. Debate rages within the medical profession as to whether "alcoholism" is a separate "disease" in any meaningful biochemical, physiological or psychological sense, or whether it represents one peculiar manifestation in some individuals of underlying psychiatric disorders ... .

... The focus at the trial, and in the dissent here, has been exclusively upon the factors of loss of control and inability to abstain. Assuming that it makes sense to compartmentalize in this manner the diagnosis of such a formless "disease," tremendous gaps in our knowledge remain, which the record in this case does nothing to fill.

The trial court's "finding" that Powell "is afflicted with the disease of chronic alcoholism," which "destroys the afflicted person's willpower to resist the constant, excessive consumption of alcohol" covers a multitude of sins. Dr. Wade's testimony that appellant suffered from a compulsion which was an "exceedingly strong influence," but which was "not completely overpowering," is at least more carefully stated, if no less mystifying. Jellinek insists that conceptual clarity can only be achieved by distinguishing carefully between "loss of control" once an individual has commenced to drink and "inability to abstain" from drinking in the first place. [Id. at 41.] Presumably, a person would have to display both characteristics in order to make out a constitutional defense, should one be recognized. Yet the "findings" of the trial court utterly fail to make this crucial distinction, and there is serious question whether the record can be read to support a finding of either loss of control or inability to abstain.

Dr. Wade did testify that, once appellant began drinking, he appeared to have no control over the amount of alcohol he finally ingested. Appellant's own testimony concerning his drinking on the day of the trial would certainly appear, however, to cast doubt upon the conclusion that he was without control over his consumption of alcohol when he had sufficiently important reasons to exercise such control. However that may be, there are more serious factual and conceptual difficulties with reading this record to show that appellant was unable to abstain from drinking. Dr. Wade testified that, when appellant was sober, the act of taking the first drink was a "voluntary exercise of his will," but that this exercise of will was undertaken under the "exceedingly strong influence" of a "compulsion" which was "not completely overpowering." Such concepts, when juxtaposed in this fashion, have little meaning ... .

... It would be tragic to return large numbers of helpless, sometimes dangerous and frequently unsanitary inebriates to the streets of our cities without even the opportunity to sober up adequately, which a brief jail term provides. Presumably no State or city will tolerate such a state of affairs. Yet the medical profession cannot, and does not, tell us with any assurance that, even if the buildings, equipment and trained personnel were made available, it could provide anything more than slightly higher-class jails for our indigent habitual inebriates. Thus, we run the grave risk that nothing will be accomplished beyond the hanging of a new sign — reading "hospital" — over one wing of the jailhouse ... .

Faced with this unpleasant reality, we are unable to assert that the use of the criminal process as a means of dealing with the public aspects of problem drinking can never be defended as rational. The picture of the penniless drunk propelled aimlessly and endlessly through the law's "revolving door" of arrest, incarceration, release and re-arrest is not a pretty one. But before we condemn the present practice across the board, perhaps we ought to be able to point to some clear promise of a better world for these unfortunate people. Unfortunately, no such promise has yet been forthcoming. If, in addition to the absence of a coherent approach to the problem of treatment, we consider the almost complete absence of facilities and manpower for the implementation of a rehabilitation program, it is difficult to say in the present context that the criminal process is utterly lacking in social value ... . The fact that a high percentage of American alcoholics conceal their drinking problems not merely by avoiding public displays of intoxication, but also by shunning all forms of treatment, is indicative that some powerful deterrent operates to inhibit the public revelation of the existence of alcoholism. Quite probably, this deterrent effect can be largely attributed to the harsh moral attitude which our society has traditionally taken toward intoxication and the shame which we have associated with alcoholism. Criminal conviction represents the degrading public revelation of what Anglo-American society has long condemned as a moral defect, and the existence of criminal sanctions may serve to reinforce this cultural taboo, just as we presume it serves to reinforce other stronger feelings against murder, rape, theft, and other forms of antisocial conduct ... .

... If Leroy Powell cannot be convicted of public intoxication, it is difficult to see how a State can convict an individual for murder if that individual, while exhibiting normal behavior in all other respects, suffers from a "compulsion" to kill which is an "exceedingly strong influence," but "not completely overpowering."

... We are unable to conclude, on the state of this record or on the current state of medical knowledge, that chronic alcoholics in general, and Leroy Powell in particular, suffer from such an irresistible compulsion to drink and to get drunk in public that they are utterly unable to control their performance of either or both of these acts, and thus cannot be deterred at all from public intoxication. And, in any event, this Court has never articulated a general constitutional doctrine of *mens rea*.

We cannot cast aside the centuries-long evolution of the collection of interlocking and overlapping concepts which the common law has

utilized to assess the moral account-
ability of an individual for his antisocial deeds. The doctrines of *actus
reus*, *mens rea*, insanity, mistake,
justification, and duress have histor-
ically provided the tools for a constantly shifting adjustment of the
tension between the evolving aims of
the criminal law and changing religious, moral, philosophical, and
medical views of the nature of man.
This process of adjustment has
always been thought to be the
province of the States.

Nothing could be less fruitful than
for this Court to be impelled into
defining some sort of insanity test in
constitutional terms ... .

•

7 Freedom of Choice

"When you stop drinking, you have to deal with this marvelous personality that started you drinking in the first place."
–Jimmy Breslin, *Table Money*

OVERCOMING AN ALCOHOL problem involves more than just learning to say, "No," or, if moderating, learning to say, "When." It typically means changing one's values and developing a whole host of new skills that can be applied to many aspects of one's life. These new values and skills must then be integrated into one's social interactions and daily routine.

For a therapist, getting a problem drinker to do all this involves a process of (1) determining whether a drinking problem exists ("screening"), (2) motivating the person to change his behavior by showing him there are incentives to change, (3) having the person take visible actions (using therapy that involves "doing" as opposed to merely "talking,"[1]) (4) using early successes to build self-esteem, and (5) maintaining harm-free behavior (in other words, preventing relapse).

While this all sounds very complicated and time-consuming, bear in mind that up to a third of all problem drinkers accomplish these tasks on their own, without formal treatment. It is certainly not easy, but people are able to help themselves — if they see sufficient reason for doing so. Often, brief treatment that focuses on just this one aspect — motivating the drinker to change her behavior — is enough to put the drinker on the path to recovery.

In some cases, however, treatment may actually make the situation worse. This is often the case when the drinker feels her recovery is wholly dependent upon only one treatment. However, if the person is aware she has options — that if one treatment fails, there are others — then setbacks along the road to recovery won't seem so catastrophic and demoralizing. Treatment is least successful when the drinker is forced into it. Again, when the person perceives she has choices and can participate in choosing, she is less likely to resist change.

In general, treatments fall into two categories: inpatient and outpatient. Each has its advantages and disadvantages. The inpatient setting removes the drinker from all the stresses of daily life and allows him to work with his therapist intensely, under close supervision.

The critics of inpatient treatment, however, have described the disadvantages thus:

> ... the most absurd way to treat problem drinkers is to take them off to a residential institution miles away — physically or psychologically — from their home community. A drinking problem does not reside in the individual but arises from the interaction between the individual and his environment. If drinkers are to resist cues for drinking they must be in contact with the environment which conveys these cues; if they are to lose conditioned tolerance, they must face up to

the stimuli of the environment in which tolerance has developed; if there is to be a change
in the incentive or "payoff" balance in favor of
abstinence or controlled drinking, that change
has to be negotiated and arranged in the
drinker's family and social environment.[2]

In its *Tenth Annual Report to Congress*, the National
Institute on Alcohol Abuse and Alcoholism clearly
favored outpatient treatment for alcoholism, citing the
following reasons:

1. Inpatient alcoholism programs lasting four weeks
   to a few months showed no higher success rates
   than did periods of brief hospitalization for a few
   days.
2. Some patients could be safely detoxified without
   pharmacotherapy and in non-hospital-based environments.
3. Partial hospitalization programs, "day hospitalization," with no overnight stays had results equal or
   superior to inpatient hospitalization at one-half to
   one-third the cost.
4. In some populations, outpatient programs produced results comparable to those of inpatient
   programs.[3]

Although outpatient treatment has the advantages of
lower cost and less disruption to the patient's daily life,
hospital inpatient treatment is usually beneficial for (1)
patients in the midst of severe withdrawal (the DTs); (2)
those who suffer from concurrent medical or psychiatric problems; (3) people who fall below the poverty
line; and (4) those who do not have strong community
or family ties.

Inpatient treatment can cost nearly $600 a day, rep-
resenting the most expensive treatment option.

Individual psychotherapy costs, on average, $1,000 for the typical length of treatment. Attendance at self-help groups such as AA costs the least (members are only encouraged, but not required, to make small donations).

Cost aside, when evaluating treatment options, it is important to look beyond the person's change in drinking behavior. A person who achieves abstinence at the cost of his job, marriage, freedom from jail, and physical health may have paid too high a price for that "achievement." Success, therefore, is not merely a matter of abstinence if the person's relationships, health, and employability continue to deteriorate. Other factors to consider are daily and monthly alcohol consumption, physical health, relationship with family and friends, residential status, legal troubles, job stability, and financial status. Thus, a "failure to abstain" is hardly a failure at all if the person has markedly decreased his alcohol consumption, improved his marital situation, found stable employment, and reports good health. To admonish a person who has achieved such improvements for failing to abstain can be counterproductive.

The treatments described in this chapter are summaries of those detailed in *The Handbook of Alcoholism Treatment Approaches*.[4] The editors of this guide for professional therapists reviewed 219 alcohol treatment outcome studies, selecting each by the following criteria:

1. The study included at least one treatment intended to affect problematic alcohol consumption.

2. The study compared the treatments with a control condition or with any alternative treatments.

3. A proper procedure (e.g., randomization, case control matching) was used to equate groups prior to

treatment.

4. The study included at least one outcome measure of drinking and/or of alcohol-related problems.

Using these criteria, the editors evaluated forty-three treatment methods and ranked them by outcome and cost-effectiveness. Briefly described below are the most effective methods, which, as the editors point out, are not necessarily the ones most widely used: "The negative correlation between scientific evidence and application in standard practice remains striking, and could hardly be larger if one intentionally constructed treatment programs from those approaches with the *least* evidence of efficacy ... . We believe that the best hope lies in assembling a menu of effective alternatives, and then seeking a system for finding the right combination of elements for each individual."[5]

As is clear from each description, many aspects of the following approaches overlap or are meant to be used in conjunction with other treatments. Comprehensive alcohol treatment programs usually involve seven stages: screening, diagnosis, assessment, motivation, treatment, planning, and follow-up. Some treatment approaches involve all seven steps; some approaches realize good outcomes by focusing on only one step. The following approaches are presented in order of where they would fall among the seven stages.

Screening

Screening services by themselves may help make a drinker aware that he has a problem and provide him with a referral to more complete services. Although studies have shown that only 10 to 15 percent of people who receive referrals to alcohol treatment programs ever actually use them,[6] this is probably because most referrals are given as mandates by legal or medical authorities, with no discussion of treatment options. When screening is conducted in a less threatening environment, follow-through tends to improve.

Such assessment typically involves determining (1) the client's own understanding of the alcohol problems; (2) the potential consequences of continuing the current level of drinking; (3) his or her willingness to participate in assessment and possible treatment for alcohol problems; (4) various options related to dealing with the drinking behavior; and (5) how family members and friends might react to his or her undertaking a comprehensive alcohol assessment.[7]

The *Handbook* recommends incorporating alcohol-screening procedures into an annual physical: "This allows questions or concerns about alcohol use to be discussed in the language of health promotion rather than disease detection. Avoid reference to disease labels such as 'alcoholism' and 'alcoholic.' You want to convey to the client that there are potential health risks associated with drinking, and that, based on the information gathered in the screening test, you need to determine whether the client is at-risk for such problems."[8]

Motivational Enhancement

In the traditional, AA view, alcoholics do not develop the motivation to change their drinking habits until they have hit "rock bottom." If they are forced into treatment before reaching this point, their lack of motivation may be blamed on "denial." Therapists specializing in motivational enhancement, however, argue that waiting for a drinker to hit a low point or seeing "denial" as an impenetrable blockade are unnecessary: "Motivation is now understood to be the result of an *interaction* between the drinker and those around him or her. This means that there are things a therapist can do to increase motivation for change."[9]

When an individual — drinker or teetotaler — considers changing a deeply ingrained habit, he weighs the pros and cons of doing so. Assessing the effort involved and the potential for improvement are the beginning stages of making any change. The change process has been described as a series of stages: pre-contemplation, contemplation, determination, action, maintenance, and relapse.[10]

Once the person has initiated a change, staying motivated to maintain the new behavior is arguably the most difficult stage. It's easier to initially lose weight, for example, than to keep it off. Or, as the saying goes, "Quitting is easy — I've done it a thousand times!" Sustaining motivation over the long term is the challenge. How one responds to a relapse or a setback, then, is very important to one's overall goal of improvement. The quicker the recovery from a relapse, the less likely the drinker will have to start right back at square one.

People's motivation increases when they see how alcohol is affecting them personally — not just generally. The *Handbook* points out that general educational materials such as lectures and films about the potentially harmful effects of alcohol have little or no impact on drinking behavior, either in treatment or in prevention settings. A therapist providing personal feedback regarding ways in which alcohol actually is harming the individual currently, however, tends to have a strong motivational effect.[11]

Effective motivational techniques also emphasize the client's personal responsibility and freedom of choice. Writing in the *Handbook*, William R. Miller, professor and director of the University of New Mexico's Center on Alcoholism, Substance Abuse, and Addictions, explains:

> Rather than giving restrictive messages (you have to, can't, must, etc.), the counselor acknowledges that ultimately it is up to the client whether or not to change ... .
>
> ... counseling methods that effectively get people moving on a course of action have frequently offered a variety of alternative strategies for change. There is a predictable outcome in telling an ambivalent (contemplator) person that there is only one thing to do: 'Yes, but ... ' Better to say something like this: 'There are several different ways that people have successfully changed their drinking. Let me tell you about some of them and you can tell me which of these might make the most sense for you.' Again, the client is actively involved in choosing his or her own approach.[12]

Several studies have illustrated the beneficial effects of choice. One researcher divided people with drinking problems into two groups. Each group was exposed to one of four types of treatment, each ranging in intensity. The people in the first group were asked to choose which of the four treatments they wanted, whereas the people in the second group were assigned to one of the four treatments. The people who were allowed to choose their treatment were much more likely to work hard to solve their problem than those who were not and were more likely to ask for additional help if they needed it than were those in the second group. The people who were forced into a treatment that they did not choose were less likely to solve their problem, more likely to drop out of treatment, and less likely to seek additional help even though they might need some.[13]

Needless to say, in order to motivate a client, a therapist must believe that change is possible and convey that belief to the client. Unfortunately, professionals working within conventional treatment programs tend to give up optimism when confronted with a client's "denial." Dr. Miller argues, "The resistant behavior that is labeled 'denial' does not just walk through the door with the client, but is strongly influenced by the way in which the therapist approaches the client. Said provocatively, denial is not a client problem. It is a therapist problem."[14]

Instead of allowing an impasse to form over the client's denial, motivational therapists seek to negotiate with the client a change strategy based on several options. The therapist then is "not in the position of 'selling' a single particular approach, thus running the risk of evoking client resistance ... . The choice process increases the client's perception of personal control and enhances motivation for compliance."[15]

Even when the therapist believes abstinence is the best goal for the client, arguing about it may be futile and unproductive. The *Handbook* advises therapists, "There is little sense in losing a client by a standoff on this issue. There appears to be no strong relationship between a client's prognosis and his or her beliefs about the necessity of abstinence."[16]

Brief Interventions

Brief interventions scored the highest of all the treatment approaches evaluated by the *Handbook* editors. The NIAAA endorses the use of brief interventions, asserting that when patients are found to be at-risk or problem drinkers, but not alcohol-dependent, health care providers can reduce alcohol use and related problems significantly by providing brief interventions. Brief interventions can take many forms, but basically consist of feedback and advice from the health care provider and agreement by the patient on a course of action.[17]

In a brief intervention, the general practitioner essentially does the following:

1. States the medical concern.
2. Advises the patient to abstain from alcohol use, if alcohol dependent, or to cut down if not.
3. Agrees on a plan of action — this may be done by negotiating with the patient an informal contract or agreement that sets specific goals, such as a certain number of drinks per week.[18]

The general practitioner can also offer patients techniques to help them modify their behavior, for example, having patients list the situations in which they typically lose control of their drinking, then helping them to devise ways to avoid those situations.

How brief is a brief intervention? Two or three sessions of assessment, advice, or counseling is usually sufficient.[19] Brief interventions, however, may not be sufficient for people with severe dependency problems. Because they are normally directed at problem drinkers with only low or moderate levels of alcohol dependence or alcohol-related problems, most brief interventions aim for a goal of moderate or harm-free drinking rather than total abstinence.

If the client asks the therapist to recommend either abstinence or moderation, assessing the drinker's level of dependence, therefore, is crucial. Therapists have a number of instruments available for doing so: the Severity of Alcohol Dependence Questionnaire (SADQ), the Alcohol Dependence Scale (ADS), the Short-Form Alcohol Dependence Data Questionnaire (SADD), pH score from the Comprehensive Drinker Profile (CDP), and the Edinburgh Alcohol Dependence Scale (EADS), to name just a few.[20]

For drinkers who display a high level of dependence, the *Handbook* advises pursuing intensive treatment aimed at abstinence. However, if the client rejects all advice aimed at abstinence, then the therapist should certainly make every effort to help him to drink at safer levels.[21]

Behavioral Self-Control Training

Behavioral self-control training (BSCT) teaches techniques for goal-setting, self-monitoring, managing consumption, rewarding goal attainment, analyzing drinking situations, and learning alternate coping skills.[22] It can support a goal of abstinence or moderate, harm-free drinking.

According to BSCT therapists, when moderation is the goal, "we agree to work with the client for six to eight weeks, providing them training in BSCT. We agree, however, that if at the end of that time the client is still having difficulty drinking moderately, he or she will consider a goal of abstinence."[23]

There are various protocols for BSCT: Miller and Munoz's *How to Control Your Drinking*, Robertson and

Heather's *Let's Drink to Your Health*, Sanchez-Craig's *Saying When: How to Quit Drinking or Cut Down*, and the Sobells' *Problem Drinkers: Guided Self-Change Treatment*.[24]

The *Handbook* describes BSCT as involving the following eight steps:

1. Setting limits on the number of drinks per day and on peak blood alcohol concentrations.
2. Self-monitoring of drinking behaviors.
3. Changing the rate of drinking.
4. Practicing assertiveness in refusing drinks.
5. Setting up a reward system for achievement of goals.
6. Learning which antecedents result in over-drinking and which in moderation.
7. Learning other coping skills instead of drinking.
8. Learning how to avoid relapsing back into heavy drinking.[25]

Before they begin drinking, clients fill out an information card that includes the day, time, type of drink, amount of alcohol in the drink, place of drinking, and with whom they are drinking. Writing down the data on each drink makes them aware of how long it has been since their last drink and how many drinks they have already had that day.[26]

BSCT clients are also encouraged to switch from stronger drinks (i.e., hard liquor) to weaker drinks (i.e., beer or wine). Learning to drink more slowly by putting the glass down between sips is another helpful technique.[27]

Clients are also encouraged to give themselves rewards for reaching or maintaining goals. The trick is to time the rewards as soon as possible after the achievement. The *Handbook* explains, "A trip to Hawaii next year for success this week is not a timely reward.

Rewards involving time (especially for busy clients) might include an hour of doing absolutely nothing or taking the time to read a favorite book ... .A penalty should be something that the client genuinely dislikes but is in some way constructive. Examples might include cleaning out the garage or picking up litter in the neighborhood."[28]

Rather than ignoring the positive consequences of drinking that the clients perceive, BSCT therapists help clients to brainstorm other ways to achieve the desired effects without overdrinking.[29]

Coping and Social Skills Training

Coping and social skills training (CSST) imparts four major skills:

1. Interpersonal skills for building better relationships
2. Cognitive emotional coping for mood regulation
3. Coping skills for improving daily living and dealing with stressful life events
4. Coping in the context of substance use cues[30]

Similar to BSCT, CSST teaches self-monitoring, goal-setting, coping and social skills training, self-evaluation, and self-correction. The therapist negotiates the goals of treatment with the client, and together they practice using new skills and evaluating the client's progress.

In either group or individual settings, clients learn the skills necessary to avoid drinking situations, to cope with stressful situations, and to deal with spouses, children, bosses, and other relationships. Managing anger, relaxing, identifying and modifying negative thinking, being assertive, and articulating needs are important aspects of CSST.

The *Handbook* found CSST to be effective with a more severely alcohol-dependent population than were brief interventions.[31]

Self-Help Groups

The success of Alcoholics Anonymous has spawned twelve-step programs for almost every possible compulsion: Gambler's Anonymous, Shopaholics Anonymous, Workaholics Anonymous, and self-help groups for sex addicts, shoplifters, overeaters, women who love too much, and others who suffer from compulsive behavioral disorders. As discussed in Chapter 2, these twelve-step programs draw on spiritual techniques derived from the temperance movement and nineteenth-century Protestant revivalism. The steps involve public confession, submission to a Higher Power, and a commitment to a new way of life. Participation in these groups is the non-denominational equivalent of being "born again."

While researchers have difficulty evaluating the benefits of AA due to members' adherence to anonymity, AA's own membership surveys reveal that most people — 90 to 95 percent — who begin attending AA drop out within a year. Abstinence rates for regularly attending AA members vary between 25 and 50 percent at one-year follow-up.[32]

The twelve steps of AA are:

1. We admitted we were powerless over alcohol — that our lives became unmanageable.
2. We came to believe that a Power greater than ourselves could restore us to sanity.
3. We made a decision to turn our will and our lives

over to the care of God as we understood Him.

4. We made a searching and fearless moral inventory of ourselves.

5. We admitted to God, to ourselves, and to another human being the exact nature of our wrongs.

6. We were entirely ready to have God remove all these defects of character.

7. We humbly asked Him to remove our shortcomings.

8. We made a list of all persons we had harmed, and became willing to make amends to them all.

9. We made direct amends to such people wherever possible, except when to do so would injure them or others.

10. We continued to take personal inventory and when we were wrong we promptly admitted it.

11. We sought through prayer and meditation to improve our conscious contact with God, as we understood Him, praying only for knowledge of His will for us and the power to carry that out.

12. Having had a spiritual awakening as the result of these steps, we tried to carry this message to alcoholics, and to practice these principles in all our affairs.

Note that, although AA takes the position that alcoholism is a disease, the twelve steps do not mention sickness; instead they focus on God, "defects of character," "moral inventory," and "spiritual awakening."

AA operates its groups based on the following "Twelve Traditions":

1. Our common welfare should come first; personal recovery depends upon AA unity.

2. For our group purpose there is but one ultimate authority — a loving God as he may express Himself in our group conscience. Our leaders are

but trusted servants; they do not govern.

3. The only requirement for AA membership is a desire to stop drinking.

4. Each group should be autonomous except in matters affecting other groups or AA as a whole.

5. Each group has but one primary purpose — to carry its message to the alcoholic who still suffers.

6. An AA group ought never endorse, finance, or lend the AA name to any related facility or outside enterprise, lest problems of money, property, and prestige divert us from our primary purpose.

7. Every AA group ought to be fully self-supporting, declining outside contributions.

8. AA should remain forever non-professional, but our service centers may employ special workers.

9. AA, as such, ought never be organized; but we may create service boards or committees directly responsible for those they serve.

10. AA has no opinion on outside issues; hence the AA name ought never be drawn into public controversy.

11. Our public relations policy is based on attraction rather than promotion; we need always maintain personal anonymity at the level of press, radio, and films.

12. Anonymity is the spiritual foundation of all our traditions, ever reminding us to place principles before personalities.

AA conducts open meetings, which newcomers and outsiders are welcome to attend, and closed meetings for members only. Open meetings typically begin with a reading of the twelve steps and a roll call of "anniversaries," during which attendees proclaim they've been sober for three days, three weeks, three years, or the like. During open meetings, a speaker may tell her story, after which attendees may share their similar experiences. Closed meetings often discuss a particular topic, step, or passage in the so-called "Big Book," formally titled *Alcoholics Anonymous.* New members are often assigned sponsors who can share their experiences on a one-to-one basis and make themselves available day or night by phone for moral support.

The *Handbook* reports that, as of 1995, "only three studies have reported the results of randomized clinical trials that included AA. All three studies were conducted using coerced populations — chronic drunkenness offenders, persons convicted of DWI, employees referred to an employee assistance program. Because AA is intended to be a voluntary program open to persons with a desire to stop drinking, evaluating its effectiveness with persons who are required to attend and who do not necessarily want to stop drinking does not provide a fair test of its effectiveness ... . Overall, none of the controlled trials found AA to be more effective than alternative treatment."[33]

Self-help group alternatives to the twelve-step method include the Calix Society, an abstinence-oriented program for Catholics; the Secular Organizations for Sobriety (SOS), which separate religion or spirituality from sobriety and support a scientific approach to recovery; Women for Sobriety, which addresses the needs of women; and Moderation Management, SMART Recovery, and Rational Recovery, which are described in detail below.

Moderation Management. Moderation Management (MM) is a support group that encourages members to accept personal responsibility for choosing and maintaining their own path, whether moderation or abstinence. Based on a nine-step program, MM groups provide information about alcohol, moderate drinking guidelines and limits, drink-monitoring exercises, goal-setting techniques, and self-management strategies. As a major part of the program, members learn to apply the nine steps to many other areas of their lives.

MM emphatically warns that the program is not for drinkers who experience significant withdrawal symptoms when they stop drinking. It is also not intended for formerly dependent drinkers who are now abstaining.

According to its literature, "MM recognizes problem drinking as a learned behavior, not a disease, and that people who drink too much can suffer from varying degrees of alcohol-related problems, ranging from mild to moderate to severe. It sees moderation as a reasonable early option for problem drinkers and recommends abstinence for seriously dependent drinkers."

While MM members are encouraged to take personal responsibility for their own recovery from a drinking problem, they believe that "people helping people" is the strength of the organization. Like AA members, they believe that people who help others to recover also help themselves. They see self-esteem and self-management as central to recovery.

The nine steps of Moderation Management are:

1. Attend meetings (local groups or online) and learn about the program of Moderation Management.
2. Abstain from alcoholic beverages for thirty days and complete steps three through six during this time.
3. Examine how drinking has affected your life.
4. Write down your life priorities.
5. Take a look at how much, how often, and under what circumstances you used to drink.
6. Learn the MM guidelines and limits for moderate

drinking. (This information is provided at meetings and in MM literature.)

7. Set moderate drinking limits and start weekly "small steps" toward positive lifestyle changes.
8. Review your progress and update your goals.
9. Continue to make positive lifestyle changes, help newcomers to the group, and attend meetings as needed for ongoing support.

The MM Guidelines state that a moderate drinker:

- considers an occasional drink to be a small, though enjoyable, part of life.
- has hobbies, interests, and other ways to relax and enjoy life that do not involve alcohol.
- usually has friends who are moderate drinkers or nondrinkers.
- generally has something to eat before, during, or soon after drinking.
- usually does not drink for longer than an hour or two on any particular occasion.
- usually does not drink faster than one drink per half-hour.
- usually does not exceed the .055 percent blood alcohol concentration moderate drinking limit.
- feels comfortable with his or her use of alcohol (never drinks secretly and does not spend a lot of time thinking about drinking or planning to drink).

MM cautions members against drinking every day and suggests that members abstain from drinking alcohol at least three or four days per week. The drinking limits for women are no more than three drinks on any day, and no more than nine drinks per week. For men, the limits are no more than four drinks on any day, and no more than fourteen drinks per week.

Self-Management and Recovery Training (SMART). SMART Recovery is an abstinence-based nonprofit organization with a self-help program for people having problems with drinking and using drugs. The program teaches common-sense, self-help procedures designed to empower the individual to abstain and develop a healthier lifestyle. Group meetings, at which a trained professional is usually present, focus on coping with urges; managing thoughts, feelings, and behaviors; and balancing momentary and enduring pleasures. Unlike AA, SMART meetings do not dwell on participants' past "war stories," nor do they encourage participants to think of themselves as diseased or powerless.

Rational Recovery. Founded in 1986 by social worker and former problem drinker Jack Trimpey, Rational Recovery (RR) is based on the principles of rational emotive therapy (RET), which teaches clients to recognize and change irrational thoughts and beliefs that hinder them from reaching their goals.[34] (SMART Recovery, described above, also uses RET principles.)

RR offered a network of self-help groups until recently; now it offers educational programs instead. The RR program generally attracts people who have previously tried AA, but who objected to its spiritual component, its notion that the drinker is powerless, its lack of scientific grounding, or its insistence on a lifetime commitment to the program. Indeed, RR suggested that its members attend its erstwhile meetings for no more than a year. (The educational program is similarly limited in duration.) Like AA, however, the goal of the RR program is abstinence.

Realizing one's self-esteem is integral to the program. According to Trimpey, "The charge that when an alcoholic seeks help for his problem he is admitting powerlessness is simply not true. Reaching out for help is, in itself, a powerful act of self-determination."[35] (Indeed, researchers have found that drinkers who simply make appointments for alcohol-related therapy often report improvements in their lives even before their first session.[36] It appears, therefore, that merely deciding definitively to make improvements to one's life produces real and psychological benefits.)

Relapse Prevention

Relapse, or a temporary return to the problematic behavior, is practically inevitable — whether one is abstaining from alcohol, dieting, or quitting smoking. Most relapses tend to occur within the first month of changing one's habits. A relapse, however, need not be a severe, long-term episode. Problem drinkers who look upon a relapse as a learning experience, instead of as the end of the world, are more likely to achieve their long-term goals of either abstinence or moderation.

According to the *Handbook*, Relapse Prevention (RP) combines behavioral skills training procedures with cognitive techniques to help individuals maintain their desired behavioral change.[37] RP focuses on three areas:

1. Anticipating and preventing relapses from occurring,
2. Coping humanely and effectively with a relapse to minimize its negative consequences and outcome and maximize learning from the experience, and
3. Reducing global health risks and replacing lifestyle imbalance with balance and moderation.

Most RP treatment programs consist of approximately eight formal sessions and several follow-up sessions. They can supplement other treatment approaches, such as AA or inpatient treatment.

RP recognizes that problem drinkers' beliefs about

alcoholism can affect their treatment outcomes. Attitudes may stem from the moral model, for example, which assumes the individual is responsible both for the development of the addiction and for changing or failing to change the addictive behavior.[38] In this model, relapse is attributed to a lack of willpower or insufficient "moral fiber." The *Handbook* notes that this perspective often results in a "blaming the victim" mentality.[39] By contrast, the disease model places blame on a genetic or physiological defect that is outside the alcoholic's control. With this belief, "the addict forever fears the resurgence of the uncontrollable disease," in other words, a relapse.

RP advocates the "compensatory model," which posits that "the individual 'compensates' for a problem not of his or her own making by assuming active responsibility and self-mastery in the change process. Relapse is reviewed as a mistake or error in the new learning."[40] This model emphasizes the individual's power and influence in the process of change.

Coping effectively after a relapse builds a person's sense of self-efficacy and his confidence in his ability to negotiate high-risk situations in the future.[41]

Harm Reduction. Relapse Prevention is grounded in the principles of a movement known as "harm reduction." According to University of Washington professor of psychology G. Alan Marlatt, one of its staunchest proponents, "harm reduction is founded on a set of pragmatic principles and compassionate strategies designed to minimize the harmful consequences of personal drug use and associated high-risk behaviors."[42] Conceived in the 1980s in response to the rising risk of HIV transmission among injection drug users, harm reduction appealed to countries such as the Netherlands that recognized the need for a more pragmatic approach to the problem.[43] According to Dr. Marlatt,

> Rather than setting abstinence as a high-threshold requirement or precondition for receiving addiction treatment or other assistance, advocates of harm reduction are willing to reduce such barriers — thereby making it easier for those in need to "get on board," to get involved, and to get started. Low-threshold programs do this by several means: by reaching out and achieving partnership and cooperation with the targeted population in developing new programs and services; by reducing the stigma associated with getting help for these kinds of problems; and by providing an integrative, normalized approach to high-risk substance use and sexual practices.
>
> ... supporters of a low-threshold approach are willing to meet the individual on his or her own terms — to "meet you where you are" rather than "where you should be" ... .
>
> Harm reduction is based on the tenets of compassionate pragmatism versus moralistic idealism ... [It asks,] What can be done to reduce the harm and suffering for both the individual and society? Pragmatism does not ask whether the behavior in question is right or wrong, good or bad, sick or well. Pragmatism is concerned with the management of everyday affairs and actual practices, and its validity is assessed by practical results.[44]

The Harm Reduction Coalition (HRC), based in New

York City, is committed to reducing drug-related harm among individuals and communities by initiating and promoting local, regional, and national harm reduction education, interventions, and community organizing. HRC fosters alternative models to conventional health and human services and drug treatment; challenges traditional client/provider relationships; and provides resources, educational materials, and support to health professionals and drug users in their communities to address drug-related harm. Members of the coalition accept, for better and for worse, that licit and illicit drug use is part of our world and choose to work to minimize its harmful effects rather than simply ignore or condemn them.

Two notable programs conform to the principles of harm reduction and RP. One is the DrinkWise program, a behavioral self-management approach designed for problem drinkers who are not severely dependent on alcohol. The program, available in group, individual, or telephone self-help formats, takes approximately seven weeks to complete. (See "Resources" for more information about DrinkWise.) The other program, Guided Self-Change Treatment, provides skills training for problem drinkers who choose moderation goals.[45]

The Community Reinforcement Approach

The Community Reinforcement Approach (CRA) combines motivational enhancement and behavioral techniques. CRA therapists use positive reinforcement rather than confrontation. The *Handbook* explains, for example, "instead of routinely presenting the message, 'You're an alcoholic and you should never drink again,' the CRA therapist begins by asking questions about *why* an individual is drinking, and by identifying the client's reinforcement systems."[46] Training ranges from improving communication skills and job-search strategies to developing new interests to replace drinking and repairing important relationships. CRA can support goals of abstinence or moderation.

The *Handbook* reports that CRA has been proven effective for people whose alcohol problems range from mild to severe and cites at least three studies that have demonstrated that CRA is superior to standard treatment procedures.[47]

A unique component of CRA is its functional analysis, which looks at the client's drinking and non-drinking behaviors. The analysis shows the client that he or she already enjoys positive, beneficial activities that do not involve drinking. Expanding these activities is one of the goals of treatment.[48] In addition, CRA also employs the "happiness scale," which asks the client to rank his or her happiness with respect to the following factors: drinking/sobriety, job or educational progress, money management, social life, personal habits, marriage/family relationships, legal issues, emotional life, communication, and general happiness.[49]

Instead of drawing the problem drinker into a new community of people struggling with their addictions (as AA does), CRA seeks to repair the individual's ties to his existing community, drawing on the support of family and friends. CRA advocate Stanton Peele explains, " ... CRA galvanizes forces in the alcoholic's life to reinforce sobriety and discourage further drinking. For example, the therapy trains a drinker's wife simply to lock the drinker out if he comes home drunk, until he knows unambiguously that his wife refuses to accept the drinking and what will be the consequences if he continues his drunkenness."[50]

Dr. Peele also observes, "One great paradox in America is that so many of us are willing to join self-help groups and movements and yet are reluctant to be part of our own communities."[51] CRA aims to reverse that trend.

Drug Therapies

Treating alcohol addiction with drugs is considered a dubious practice at conventional treatment centers. The fear is that the addict will merely swap one addiction for another. But possibly the most effective treatment for certain problem drinkers actually is a drug — disulfiram, also known as Antabuse. This drug was discovered, quite by accident, when workers in a rubber factory became violently ill whenever they drank alcohol. In the 1940s, scientists discovered that a chemical used in rubber processing was to blame. A few years later, doctors began using that chemical for treating alcoholics.

Although it is harmless by itself, when the chemical interacts with alcohol, the drinker becomes severely ill. The mere prospect of the nausea is incentive enough to keep virtually any alcoholic from drinking. According to one doctor, "This frees patients from the struggle of deciding whether to take a drink or not, and allows them to devote their emotional energy to restructuring their lives."[52]

Disulfiram is thus an effective aversion therapy. Aversion therapies, such as electric shock, work by conditioning the drinker to associate drinking with an unpleasant reaction rather than a pleasant one.

If disulfiram is so effective, why isn't it prescribed more often? The reason is that if the person truly wants to drink, all he needs to do is simply not take his pills. So while the treatment is certainly effective, it is difficult (and expensive) to administer.

The *Handbook* reports that good candidates for disulfiram have the following characteristics: (1) a longer history of heavy drinking; (2) a history of delirium tremens; (3) good motivation for abstinence; and, (4) no existing treatment with antidepressant medications.[53] Furthermore, people taking disulfiram must be able to avoid even small amounts of alcohol that might be present in over-the-counter cold remedies and in food prepared with wine or liquor. The resulting sickness could be severe enough to require medical attention.

Researchers have experimented with numerous other drugs as potential treatments for alcoholism, even, for a short time in the 1950s, lysergic acid diethylamide-25, more commonly known as LSD. Needless to say, the side effects outweighed any benefits. More recently, the antidepressant and anti-anxiety drugs Prozac, Zoloft, and Paxil have been tried, to little avail. These drugs fall into a class known as "selective serotonin reuptake inhibitors" or SSRIs, which regulate the amount of the chemical serotonin in the brain. Experts have theorized that dependent drinkers have serotonin deficiencies, as low levels of serotonin lead to impulsive behavior, such as excessive alcohol consumption. The relative ineffectiveness of these drugs, however, calls that theory into question, although early studies suggest that the SSRI drug ondansetron may prove effective for patients with early signs of drinking problems.[54]

Substances like heroin and morphine, called opiates, act like chemicals the brain produces naturally called "endogenous opioids," which stimulate pleasurable feelings and suppress pain. Medication known as "opiate antagonists" bind with the brain's receptors for endogenous opioids, thus blocking the desired effects of opiate drugs, while having no effect themselves. Alcohol is not an opiate-like substance and researchers do not know the exact mechanism by which opiate antagonists affect drinking. Nonetheless, two such drugs show promise in treating alcohol dependence.

In 1995, naltrexone (a.k.a. ReVia) was approved by the U.S. Food and Drug Administration (FDA) for treating alcohol dependence. Another drug, nalmafene, is in the testing phase of development.[55] Studies of naltrexone showed no serious side effects, but people with liver problems should not take it (thus excluding many severely dependent, long-term drinkers). Not cheap, each daily dose costs nearly $5.

The drug acamprosate, which has been available by prescription in France since 1989, has been used to treat more than one million alcohol-dependent people. The FDA has granted acamprosate the status of an investigational new drug. Although researchers are not sure exactly how it works, it decreases voluntary alcohol intake with no effects on food and water consumption, no potential for abuse, and no side effects.

The NIAAA reports that it is currently funding a study to test acamprosate and naltrexone both alone and in combination and evaluate their use versus a placebo and in conjunction with behavioral interventions.

Will the "cure" for alcoholism come in a pill? The NIAAA thinks not: "Medications hold great promise but at present cannot replace psychological treatments for people with alcohol dependence. These two classes of treatment strategies are complementary rather than competitive, and studies suggest that pharmacologic agents may be combined effectively with skilled counseling to improve treatment outcomes."[56]

Matching Clients to Alcohol Treatments

Therapists with several treatment options at hand have sought to match clients to those treatments deemed best suited to their particular needs and mindset. They do this (1) by assigning clients to alternative treatment goals, such as abstinence or moderation; (2) by assigning clients to treatments varying in intensity, from brief intervention to long-term residential treatment; (3) by using interventions differing in content, such as a disease-oriented approach or a skill-based method; and (4) by offering various options for sustaining improvements after treatment.[57]

Matching strategies have proved effective when clients have displayed certain demographic, dependence-level, and personality characteristics. Some problem drinkers, for example, have overriding psychiatric problems that demand special attention. The *Handbook* reports, however, that "highly motivated clients with low levels of alcohol dependence and ample personal and social supports for sobriety generally do quite well regardless of the program to which they are assigned."[58]

Matching Alcohol Treatments to Client Heterogeneity (Project MATCH), a recent eight-year clinical trial sponsored by the NIAAA, tested the hypothesis that patients who were appropriately matched to treatments based on characteristics of both the patient and the therapy would have better outcomes than those who were unmatched or mismatched. Specifically, Project MATCH investigated three treatments: cognitive behavioral therapy, motivational enhancement therapy, and twelve-step facilitation. The project found that each of the therapies produced generally comparable treatment outcomes.[59]

The *Handbook* points out some of the practical considerations of matching: "'Tailoring treatment to individual needs' has long been endorsed, and most professionals and programs recognize the value and importance of matching. Yet, the fact is that very few programs even offer a range of alternative approaches, let alone match individuals to them. Though the value of matching is widely recognized, putting it into practice turns out to be much more difficult."[60]

Hung Out to Dry?

While numerous treatment approaches are effective, their scarcity and lack of publicity combine to virtually deny problem drinkers access to them. In fact, plenty of other alternative treatments for problem drinking exist, albeit with more questionable outcomes: biofeedback, relaxation training, hypnosis, marital/family therapy, acupuncture, and sensory deprivation, to name a few. Among those described in this chapter, the approaches that received the highest rankings in the *Handbook*, in order, are brief intervention, social skills training, motivational enhancement, Community Reinforcement Approach, behavior contracting, aversion therapy, Relapse Prevention, cognitive therapy, disulfiram, and Behavior Social Skills Training. While AA and other self-help groups may be as effective as these treatment approaches, too few studies that confirm their efficacy exist. Existing studies would place these groups at the bottom of the list.

Despite such a vast array of treatment approaches, no one treatment has proven very effective in all cases. When therapists match clients to treatments, outcomes should improve. *But recovery outcomes are best when problem drinkers themselves choose the type of treat-*

ment that they think will work best for them and when they pick the goal — abstinence or moderation — they believe they can reach and maintain. Making more of these treatment options available to the public, therefore, should greatly reduce the amount of suffering due to problem drinking.

•

Resources

Addiction Alternatives
http://www.addictionalternatives.com/
(310) 275-LIFE

Addiction Alternatives, based in Los Angeles, provides a specialized treatment program dedicated to helping individuals overcome their bad habits. Clients may choose a goal of abstinence or moderation. Marc F. Kern, Ph.D., combines his personal experiences of addiction with his professional training to bring answers to people suffering with addictions and unwanted habits.

Addiction Research Foundation/Centre for Addiction and Mental Health
http://www.arf.org/
(416) 595-6056

The Centre for Addiction and Mental Health is the largest mental health and addictions facility in Canada, only one of four such facilities in that field to receive designation from the World Health Organization as a Centre of Excellence. Underlying all of the Centre's efforts are two principal tasks: advancing our understanding of mental health and addiction and translating this knowledge into practical resources and tools that can be used in the Centre's programs and in the broader community. The Centre is recognized for its uniqueness and its ability to integrate biological, social, and clinical research; translate research done in a laboratory into practical treatment and tools; provide a complete continuum of care in one setting; and integrate the treatment of alcohol, drug, and mental disorders.

Al-Anon/Alateen
http://www.al-anon.org/
(888) 4AL-ANON

With meetings in 112 countries, Al-Anon helps families and friends of alcoholics recover from the effects of living with the problem drinking of a relative or friend. Alateen is a recovery program for young people. The program of recovery is adapted from Alcoholics Anonymous and is based upon the Twelve Steps, Twelve Traditions, and Twelve Concepts of Service.

Alcoholics Anonymous
http://www.alcoholics-anonymous.org/
(212) 686-1100

Alcoholics Anonymous is an international fellowship of men and women who share their experience, strength, and hope with one another to solve their common problem and help others to recover from alcoholism. AA is not allied with any sect, denomination, political group, organization, or institution. The only requirement for membership is a desire to stop drinking. (See Chapter 7 for more information.)

American Council on Alcoholism
http://www.aca-usa.org/
Help Line: (800) 527-5344

The ACA provides a coordinated approach to understanding alcoholism as a disease. ACA is a forum for addressing the complex issues of prevention, early identification, and treatment of alcoholism, as well as other related alcohol use and abuse issues. ACA provides a national information network of resources on prevention, treatment, research, education, and rehabilitation of alcoholism.

Behavior Therapy Associates
http://www.behaviortherapy.com/

Behavior Therapy Associates is an organization of psychologists providing clinical services, research, training for health care and mental health providers, and consultation to organizations and businesses. Its software programs teach moderate drinking skills and its Web site offers a list of therapists across the country who practice moderation training. The Research Division is also developing a computer-based brief motivational intervention for drinkers to help them decide whether or not to change their drinking. It will become available sometime in 2002.

Betty Ford Center
http://www.bettyfordcenter.com/
(800) 854-9211

The Betty Ford Center in Southern California provides each patient with an interdisciplinary treatment team that includes a physician, nurse, dietitian, activities therapist, counselors, continuing care counselors, case managers, pastoral care counselors, family counselors, a clinical psychologist, and a psychiatrist, if needed. Gender-specific treatment and support groups are available. Groups include grief groups, senior needs, peer groups for gay and lesbian patients, and reasonable accommodations for people with disabilities. The Center's programs are based on the foundations of the twelve-step program.

DrinkWise
http://www.med.umich.edu/drinkwise/
(888) 816-2736

DrinkWise is a brief, confidential educational program that helps clients eliminate drinking problems by reducing their drinking or stopping altogether. The clients decide which is better for them: moderation or abstinence. The program is for people with mild to moderate alcohol problems who want to eliminate the negative consequences of their drinking. DrinkWise is *not* for those who are severely dependent and require treatment approaches rather than educational ones. Offered in Michigan and North Carolina, DrinkWise has the ability to deliver the program throughout the United States using its telemedicine capacities. The following is a list of DrinkWise treatment providers:

Donna Dotson
University of Michigan Hospital
1522 Simpson Road
Ann Arbor, MI 48110

Chad Emrick, Ph.D.
President/Clinical Director
A Clinic for Self-Management Inc.
390 South Potomac Way, Unit C
Aurora, CO 80012
(303) 290-0575

Jim Goldman
Manager Faculty & Staff Services, EAP
University of Iowa
5101 Daum Hall
Iowa City, IA 52240
jim-goldman@uiowa.edu

Daryl Minicucci
8036 Merrimac Drive
Manlius, NY 13104
(315) 682-9825

Hazelden
http://www.hazelden.com/
(800) 328-9000

Hazelden is a nonprofit organization that provides rehabilitation, education, prevention, and professional services for chemical dependency and related disorders based on the twelve-step program. Located outside Minneapolis, Minnesota, Hazelden also has facilities in Illinois, New York, and Florida.

Moderation Management
http://www.moderation.org/

Moderation Management (MM) is a recovery program and national support group network for people who have made the healthy decision to reduce their drinking and make other positive lifestyle changes. MM empowers individuals to accept personal responsibility for choosing and maintaining their own recovery path, whether moderation or abstinence. MM promotes early self-recognition of risky drinking behavior, when moderation is an achievable recovery goal. Individuals who are not able to reduce their drinking successfully either find a local abstinence-only program to attend or remain in MM and choose abstinence as their goal. (See Chapter 7 for more information.)

National Council on Alcoholism and Drug Dependence
(800) 622-2255

The NCADD views alcoholism as a chronic, often fatal disease. Founded in 1944, NCADD has a network of affiliates that advocate prevention, intervention, research, and treatment and are dedicated to ridding the disease of its stigma and its sufferers from their denial and shame.

National Institute on Alcohol Abuse and Alcoholism
http://www.niaaa.nih.gov/

The National Institute on Alcohol Abuse and Alcoholism (NIAAA) supports and conducts biomedical and behavioral research on the causes, consequences, treatment, and prevention of alcoholism and alcohol-related problems. NIAAA is one of eighteen institutes that make up the National Institutes of Health (NIH), the principal biomedical research agency of the federal government.

Practical Recovery Services
http://practicalrecovery.com
(858) 453-4777

Practical Recovery Services offers customized, private, brief, or intensive treatment for any type of addictive behavior or related problem. It views addictive behavior as a bad habit, not a disease. It supports both moderation and abstinence and bases treatment services on the latest scientific knowledge. Though based in La Jolla, CA, it provides long-distance addiction counseling services by e-mail or telephone.

Rational Recovery
http://rational.org/
(530) 621-4374

Founded in 1986 by social worker and former problem drinker Jack Trimpey, Rational Recovery (RR) is based on the principles of rational emotive therapy (see Chapter 7). The RR program generally attracts people who have previously tried AA, but who objected to its spiritual component, its notion that the drinker is powerless, its lack of scientific grounding, or its insistence on a lifetime commitment to the program. Until recently, RR offered a network of self-help groups; now it offers educational programs instead. The goal of the RR program is abstinence.

Rutgers University Center of Alcohol Studies
Drinker's Risk Reduction Program

Brinkley and Adele Smithers Hall
607 Allison Road
Piscataway, NJ 08854-8001
(732) 445-0941

The Drinkers Risk Reduction Program (DRRP) is a program of the Center of Alcohol Studies Consultation and Treatment Services at Rutgers University, a group of licensed or license-eligible clinical psychologists. DRRP is designed for individuals who are concerned about their own drinking or the drinking of someone close to them. The Rutgers Center of Alcohol Studies is the oldest research institute in the United States devoted to the understanding of alcohol-related problems.

For people who are concerned about their drinking and its effect on their health and well-being, DRRP offers an assessment and brief intervention program that includes: (1) Comprehensive Drinking Assessment Program; (2) a detailed feedback interview, that includes neuropsychological testing and referral for laboratory testing; (3) help from a therapist in defining personal goals, and assistance in deciding how best to go about reaching those goals; and (4) a variety of options to help in working toward the achievement of goals.

DRRP offers programs aimed at helping reduce the health risks that drinking presents, including:

- **A Self-Change Program** in which a clinician provides the client with some assistance and guidance, but the client takes the primary role in initiating changes.

- **Behavioral Self-Control Training** in which the clinician teaches skills that will help in establishing a less risky, healthier drinking pattern. Self-Change and Behavioral Self-Control Training are available in individual or group therapy.
- **Referral Service** for those whose drinking presents more serious risks, or who are dependent on alcohol and who require more intensive help.

The DRRP program philosophy is:

- To help clients reduce the harm or potential harm caused by drinking through programs tailored to individual needs and goals.
- To work with clients toward selecting healthy goals in a responsible, safe manner.
- To treat clients as responsible decision-makers who want to make healthy decisions about drinking.
- To allow clients as much input as possible into the process of changing drinking behavior.
- To encourage and support any decision that moves clients toward healthier use of alcohol and a healthier overall lifestyle.
- To provide clients with referrals and assistance in obtaining more intensive help to change their drinking habits, should that be necessary.

Secular Organizations for Sobriety

http://www.secularhumanism.org/sos
(310) 821-8430

SOS is an alternative recovery method for those alcoholics or drug addicts who are uncomfortable with the spiritual content of widely available twelve-step programs. SOS takes a reasonable, secular approach to recovery and maintains that sobriety is a separate issue from religion or spirituality. SOS credits the individual for achieving and maintaining his or her own sobriety, without reliance on any "Higher Power." SOS respects recovery in any form regardless of the path by which it is achieved. It is not opposed to or in competition with any other recovery programs. SOS supports healthy skepticism and encourages the use of the scientific method to understand alcoholism.

Self-Management and Recovery Training (SMART)

7537 Mentor Avenue, Suite 306
Mentor, OH 44060
(440) 951-5357
http://www.smartrecovery.org/

SMART Recovery is an abstinence-based nonprofit organization with a self-help program for people having problems with drinking and using drugs. The program teaches common-sense self-help procedures designed to empower the individual to abstain and develop a healthier lifestyle. SMART Recovery believes the problem drinker is neither diseased nor powerless. SMART groups meet in person or online.

**Substance Abuse and Mental Health
Services Administration
Center for Substance Abuse Treatment
Referral Service**
(800) 662-HELP
http://www.samhsa.gov/

The Center for Substance Abuse Treatment (CSAT) of
the Substance Abuse and Mental Health Services
Administration (SAMHSA), U.S. Department of Health
and Human Services (DHHS), was created in October
1992 with a congressional mandate to expand the
availability of effective treatment and recovery services
for alcohol and drug problems. CSAT's initiatives and
programs are based on research findings and the general consensus of experts in the addiction field. They
take the position that, for most individuals, treatment
and recovery work best in a community-based, coordinated system of comprehensive services. Because no
single treatment approach is effective for all persons,
CSAT supports the nation's effort to provide multiple
treatment modalities, evaluate treatment effectiveness,
and use evaluation results to enhance treatment and
recovery approaches.

The Center for Substance Abuse Prevention's mission
is to improve the quality and availability of prevention,
treatment, and rehabilitation services.

SAMHSA's online version of the most recent National
Directory of Drug Abuse and Alcoholism Treatment
Programs lists federal, state, local, and private facilities
that provide drug abuse and alcoholism treatment services that meet individual specifications.

The National Clearinghouse for Alcohol and Drug Information (NCADI), *http://www.health.org/*, is the information service of the Center for Substance Abuse Prevention of the Substance Abuse and Mental Health Services Administration in the U.S. Department of Health and Human Services. NCADI is the world's largest resource for current information and materials concerning substance abuse.

Women for Sobriety
http://www.womenforsobriety.org/
(800) 333-1606

Women for Sobriety is a nonprofit organization in Quakertown, PA, dedicated to helping women overcome alcoholism and other addictions. The "New Life" program, based on a philosophy of positivity that encourages emotional and spiritual growth, helps women to achieve abstinence and learn an entirely new lifestyle to sustain ongoing recovery. The organization boasts hundreds of self-help groups across the country.

Therapists in private practice who provide moderation training:

Raymond Anderson, Ph.D.
The Life Link, Inc.
1225 S. St. Francis Drive, Suite C
Santa Fe, NM 87505
(505) 820-7605
carollink@aol.com

Patricia Bellucci, Ph.D.
St. Luke's/Roosevelt Hospital
316 West 82nd Street, Basement Level
New York, NY 10024
(212) 787-3985

Tony Cellucci, Ph.D.
ISU Psychology Clinic
Graveley Hall North, Third Floor
Box 8021
Pocatello, ID 83209
(208) 236-2129
Cellanth@isu.edu

George H. Davis, Ph.D.
103 Whitney Avenue, Suite 4
New Haven, CT 06501
(203) 787-3070
george.davis@snet.net

William J. Dubin, Ph.D.
Psychological Assessment Research and Treatment
    Services
4131 Spicewood Springs Rd., Suite E-2
Austin, TX 78759
(512) 343-8307
bill@psycharts.com
http://www.alcohol-drug.com

David F. Duncan
Brown University Medical School
Box G-BH
Providence, RI 02912
(401) 863-2923
dduncan@brownvm.brown.edu

Chad Emrick, Ph.D.
President/Clinical Director
A Clinic for Self-Management Inc.
390 South Potomac Way, Unit C
Aurora, CO 80012
(303) 290-0575

Monda Freeman, LICSW
581 Boylston St., Ste 403
Boston, MA 02116
(617) 527-9426
priorco@aol.com

Frank J. Gold, Ed.D.
AK Associates
3098 Airport Way
Fairbanks, AK 99709
(907) 474-9292
akgold@alaska.net

Raymond Hanbury, Ph.D.
Brielle Hills Professional Park
Building 7A, Suite 202
2640 Highway 70
Manasquan, NJ 08736-2609
(732) 223-1242

Reid K. Hester, Ph.D.
Director, Research Division
Behavior Therapy Associates
3810 Osuna Rd. NE, Suite 1
Albuquerque, NM 87109
(505) 342-2474
rhester@behaviortherapy.com

Arthur T. Horvath, Ph.D., ABPP
Center for Cognitive Therapy
8950 Villa La Jolla Drive, Suite 1130
La Jolla, CA 92037-1705
(858) 455-0042

Richard J. Kelliher, Psy.D.
Director
A Center for Cognitive Therapy
22 West Mission Street, Suite C
Santa Barbara, CA 93101
(805) 687-8021

Marc F. Kern, Ph.D.
Addiction Alternatives
A Division of Life Management Skills, Inc.
Beverly Hills Medical Tower
1125 S. Beverly Drive #401
Los Angeles, CA 90035
(310) 275-5433 and
Xerox Center
1851 E. First Street, #840
Santa Ana, CA 92705
(714) 550-9311
habitdoc@addictionalternatives.com
http://www.addictionalternatives.com

Stephen A. Lisman, Ph.D.
Susquehanna Psychological Affiliates
240 Riverside Drive
Johnson City, NY 13790
(607) 797-1652
slisman@binghamton.edu

Gloria M. Miele, Ph.D.
52 Riverside Drive, 1A
New York, NY 10024
(917) 742-5478
gmm23@columbia.edu

Lisa Najavits, Ph.D.
Proctor House III
McLean Hospital
115 Mill St.
Belmont, MA 02478
(617) 855-3718
lnajavits@hms.harvard.edu

Stanton Peele, Ph.D.
27 West Lake Blvd.
Morristown, New Jersey 07960
(973) 538-0430
speele@earthlink.net
http://www.peele.net

Robert Rhode, Ph.D.
3701 E. Camino de Jaime
Tucson, AZ 85718-7435
(520) 615-7263
RRhode@U.Arizona.edu

Harold Rosenberg
Psychology Department
Bowling Green State University
Bowling Green, OH 43403
(419) 372-2540
hrosenb@bgnet.bgsu.edu

Frederick Rotgers, Psy.D.
Brielle Hills Professional Park
Building 7A, Suite 202
2640 Highway 70
Manasquan, NJ 08736-2609
(732) 223-1242
fred_etoh@yahoo.com

Edward (Ned) M. Rubin, Psy.D.
Behavioral Consultants
1428 N. Farwell Avenue, #212
Milwaukee, WI 53202
erubin@facstaff.wisc.edu.
(414) 271-5577

Jeffrey A. Schaler, Ph.D.
1001 Spring Street, Suite 1126
Silver Spring, MD 20910
(301) 585-5664
jschale@american.edu
http://www.schaler.net

Lynn E. Simons, Psy.D.
Behavioral Medicine Associates of MidMichigan, P.C.
2708 N. Saginaw Rd
Midland, MI 48640
(517) 832-9161

Linda Sobell, Ph.D.'s Guided Self-Change Clinic
Nova Southeastern University
Community Mental Health Center
Maltz Psychology Building
3301 College Ave.
Fort Lauderdale, FL 33314-7796
(954) 262-5968
gsc@cps.nova.edu

Mark Sobell, Ph.D.
Center for Psychological Studies
Nova Southeastern University
3301 College Ave
Fort Lauderdale, FL 33314
(954) 452-7201
sobellm@cps.nova.edu

Henry Steinberger, Ph.D.
Capitol Square Associates
660 West Washington Avenue, Suite 305
Madison, WI 53703
(608) 256-5176
hsteinberger@earthlink.net

Andrew Tatarsky, Ph.D., CSAS, CAS
31 West 11th Street, #6D
New York, NY 10011
(212) 633-8157
Atatarsky@aol.com

Coco Wellington, MA, LMHC, CAS, CADAC
57 Rangeley Road
Chestnet Hill, MA 02467
(617) 232-7307

Henry Wright, M.S.
Henry Wright & Associates
2505 South 17th St.
Wilmington, NC 28401
(910) 792-0022

•

Further Reading

Andrew Barr, *Drink: A Social History of America* (Carroll & Graf, 1999).

Douglas Cameron, *Liberating Solutions to Alcohol Problems* (New Jersey: Jason Aronson, Inc., 1995).

Herbert Fingarette, *Heavy Drinking* (Berkeley: The University of California Press, 1988).

Nick Heather and Ian Robertson, *Controlled Drinking* (New York: Methuen, 1981).

Nick Heather and Ian Robertson, *Problem Drinking, 3rd ed.* (Oxford University Press, 1997).

Reid K. Hester and William R. Miller (eds.), *Handbook of Alcoholism Treatment Approaches, 2nd ed.* (Needham Heights, MA: Allyn & Bacon, 1995).

A. Thomas Horvath, *Sex, Drugs, Gambling, and Chocolate: A Workbook for Overcoming Addictions* (Atascadero, CA: Impact Publishers, 1999).

E.M. Jellinek, *The Disease Concept of Alcoholism* (New Haven: Hillhouse Press, 1960).

G. Alan Marlatt (ed.), *Harm Reduction* (New York: The Guilford Press, 1998).

Scott D. Miller and Insoo Kim Berg, *The Miracle Method* (New York: W.W. Norton & Company, 1995).

David B. Morris, *Illness and Culture in the Postmodern Age* (Berkeley: University of California Press, 1998).

National Institute on Alcohol Abuse and Alcoholism, *Special Report on Alcohol and Health, Tenth Edition* (NIAAA, 1999).

Stanton Peele, *Diseasing of America* (San Francisco: Jossey-Bass, 1995).

Stanton Peele, *The Meaning of Addiction: An Unconventional View* (Jossey-Bass, 1998).

Stanton Peele and Archie Brodsky, *The Truth About Addiction and Recovery* (New York: Fireside, 1992).

Stanton Peele, Charles Bufe, and Ken Ragge, *Resisting 12-Step Coercion: How to Fight Forced Participation in AA, NA, or 12-Step Treatment* (Tucson: See Sharp Press, 2000).

Thomas R. Pegram, *Battling Demon Rum* (Chicago: Ivan R. Dee, 1998).

Mark B. Sobell and Linda Sobell, *Behavioral Treatment of Alcohol Problems* (New York: Plenum Press, 1978).

Jack Trimpey, *Rational Recovery* (New York: Pocket Books, 1996).

Jack Trimpey, *The Small Book, rev. ed.* (New York: Dell Publishing, 1992).

George E. Vaillant, *The Natural History of Alcoholism Revisited* (Cambridge: Harvard University Press, 1995).

William L. White, *Slaying the Dragon: The History of Addiction Treatment and Recovery in America* (Illinois: Chestnut Health Systems, 1998).

•

Notes

Chapter 1

[1] NIAAA, citing H. Harwood, "Updating Estimates of the Economic Costs of Alcohol Abuse in the United States: Estimates, Update Methods and Data," prepared by The Lewin Group for the NIAAA, 2000.

[2] James R. Milam and Katherine Ketcham, *Under the Influence* (New York: Bantam, 1983), pp. 4-5.

[3] G. Alan Marlatt (ed.), *Harm Reduction* (New York: The Guilford Press, 1998), p. 70.

[4] George E. Vaillant, *The Natural History of Alcoholism Revisited* (Cambridge: Harvard University Press, 1995), p. 132.

[5] Vaillant, p. 40.

[6] Milam and Ketcham, p. 57.

Chapter 2

[1] Thomas R. Pegram, *Battling Demon Rum* (Chicago: Ivan R. Dee, 1998), p. 3.

[2] Nick Heather and Ian Robertson, *Problem Drinking, 2nd ed.* (Oxford University Press, 1989), p. 42.

[3] James R. Milam and Katherine Ketcham, *Under the Influence* (New York: Bantam, 1983), p. 136.

[4] Milam and Ketcham, p. 138.

[5] Philip Van Doren Stern (ed.), *The Life and Writings of Abraham Lincoln* (New York: Random House, 1940), pp. 261-266.

[6] Pegram, pp. 76-77.

[7] Stanton Peele, *Diseasing of America* (San Francisco: Jossey-Bass, 1995), p. 42, citing N.E. Zinberg and K.M. Fraser, "The Role of Social Setting in the Prevention and Treatment of Alcoholism," in *The Diagnosis and Treatment of Alcoholism*, 2nd ed., J.H. Mendelson and N.K. Mello (eds.) (New York: McGraw-Hill, 1985).

[8] Pegram, pp. 169-170.

[9] Peele, p. 44.

[10] All song lyrics from *American School Songs* (Chicago: Hope Publishing Company).

[11] *The Complete Essays and Other Writings of Ralph Waldo Emerson*, Brooks Atkinson (ed.), (New York: Random House, 1940), pp. 332-333.

Chapter 3

[1] E.M. Jellinek, "Phases in the Drinking History of Alcoholics," *Quarterly Journal of Studies on Alcohol*, v. 7 (1946), pp. 1-88; E.M. Jellinek, "Phases of Alcohol Addiction," *Quarterly Journal of Studies on Alcohol*, v. 13 (1952), pp. 673-684.

[2] E.M. Jellinek, *The Disease Concept of Alcoholism* (New Haven: Hillhouse Press, 1960).

[3] Herbert Fingarette, *Heavy Drinking* (Berkeley: The University of California Press, 1988), p. 20, citing Pattison, "Ten Years of Change in Alcoholism Treatment Findings," *American Journal of Psychiatry*, v. 134 (1977), pp. 261-266; and Rodin, "Alcoholism as a Folk Disease," *Journal of Studies on Alcohol*, v. 42 (1981), pp. 822-835.

[4] Nick Heather and Ian Robertson, *Controlled Drinking* (New York: Methuen, 1981), p. 13.

[5] Jellinek (1960), p. 159.

[6] WHO Expert Committee on Mental Health: Alcoholism Subcommittee, *Technical Report No. 48* (1952).

[7] Nick Heather and Ian Robertson, *Problem Drinking*, *3rd ed.* (Oxford University Press, 1997), p. 46.

[8] Marc A. Schuckit, M.D., "New Findings in the Genetics of Alcoholism," *Journal of the American Medical Association*, May 26, 1999.

[9] D.W. Goodwin, F. Schulzinger, N. Moller, L. Hermansen, G. Winokur, and S.B. Guze, "Drinking Problems in Adopted and Non-Adopted Sons of Alcoholics," *Archives of General Psychiatry*, v. 32 (1974), pp. 164-169.

[10] Fingarette, p. 48.

[11] Heather and Robertson (1997), p. 91.

[12] National Institute on Alcohol Abuse and Alcoholism, *Special Report on Alcohol and Health, Tenth Edition* (NIAAA, 1999), Introduction.

[13] Heather and Robertson (1997), p. 95.

[14] George E. Vaillant, *The Natural History of Alcoholism Revisited* (Cambridge: Harvard University Press, 1995), p. 7.

[15] Heather and Robertson (1997), p. 57.

[16] G. Edwards and M.M. Gross, "Alcohol Dependence: Provisional Description of a Clinical Syndrome," *British Medical Journal*, v. 1 (1976), pp. 1058-61.

[17] *The Diagnostic and Statistical Manual of Mental Disorders-IV* (American Psychiatric Association, 1994).

Chapter 4

[1] D.L. Davies, "Normal Drinking in Recovered Alcohol Addicts," *Quarterly Journal of Studies on Alcohol*, v. 24 (1962), pp. 321-332.

[2] Nick Heather and Ian Robertson, *Controlled Drinking* (New York: Methuen, 1981), p. 27.

[3] Nick Heather and Ian Robertson, *Controlled Drinking* (New York: Methuen, 1981).

[4] Nick Heather and Ian Robertson, *Problem Drinking*, 2nd ed. (Oxford University Press, 1989), pp. 92-93.

[5] D.J. Armor, J.M. Polich, and H.B. Stambul, *Alcoholism and Treatment* (Santa Monica: Rand Corporation, 1976).

[6] Nick Heather and Ian Robertson, *Problem Drinking*, 3rd ed. (Oxford University Press, 1997), p. 68.

[7] George E. Vaillant, *The Natural History of Alcoholism Revisited* (Cambridge: Harvard University Press, 1995), p. 178.

[8] K.M. Fillmore, "Relationships Between Specific Drinking Problems in Early Adulthood and Middle Age: An Exploratory 20-Year Follow-Up Study," *Journal of Studies on Alcohol*, v. 36 (1975), pp. 882-907.

[9] Vaillant, p. 178.

[10] Vaillant, p. 180.

[11] Vaillant, p. 181.

[12] G. Alan Marlatt (ed.), *Harm Reduction* (New York: The Guilford Press, 1998), p. 81.

[13] Marlatt, p. 81, citing L.C. Sobell, J.A. Cunningham, M.B. Sobell, S. Agrawal, D.R. Gavin, G. I. Leo, and K.N. Singh, "Fostering Self-Change Among Problem Drinkers: A Pro-Active Community Intervention," *Addictive Behaviors*, v. 21 (1996), pp. 817-833.

[14] Marlatt, p. 81.

[15] Heather and Robertson (1981), p. 74.

[16] N.K. Mello and J.H. Mendelson, "Operant Analysis of Drinking Habits of Chronic Alcoholics," *Nature*, v. 206 (1965), pp. 43-46; J.H. Mendelson and N.K. Mello, "Experimental Analysis of Drinking Behavior of Chronic Alcoholics," *Annals of New York Academy of Sciences*, v. 133 (1966), pp. 828-845; J.H. Mendelson, N.K. Mello, and P. Soloman, "Small Group Drinking Behavior: An Experimental Study of Chronic Alcoholics," in A. Wikler (ed.), *The Addictive States* (Baltimore: Williams and Wilkins, 1968); N.K. Mello, H.B. McNamee, and J.H. Mendelson, "Drinking Patterns of Chronic Alcoholics: Gambling and Motivation for Alcohol," *Psychiatric Research Report No. 24* (Washington, DC: American Psychiatric Association, 1968); J.H. Mendelson and N.K. Mello, "Drinking Patterns During Work-Contingent and Non-Contingent Alcohol Acquisition," *Psychosomatic Medicine*, v. 34 (1972), pp. 139-164.

[17] Heather and Robertson (1981), p. 75.

[18] Heather and Robertson (1981), pp. 86-87.

[19] M. Cohen, I.A. Liebson, and L.A. Faillace, "A Technique for Establishing Controlled Drinking in Chronic Alcoholics," *Diseases of the Nervous System*, v. 33 (1972), pp. 46-49.

[20] Heather and Robertson (1981), p. 95.

[21] E.M. Pattison, M.B. Sobell, and L.C. Sobell, *Emerging Concepts of Alcohol Dependence* (New York: Springer, 1977).

[22] *Lancet*, v. 4 (1966), pp. 1257-1258.

[23] Heather and Robertson (1981), p. 99.

[24] G.A. Marlatt, B. Demming, and J.B. Reid, "Loss of Control Drinking in Alcoholics: An Experimental Analog," *Journal of Abnormal Psychology*, v. 81 (1973), pp. 233-241.

[25] M. Keller, "On the Loss-of-Control Phenomenon in Alcoholism," *British Journal of Addiction*, v. 67 (1972), pp. 153-166; see also Heather and Robertson (1981), p. 111.

[26] Herbert Fingarette, *Heavy Drinking* (Berkeley: The University of California Press, 1988), p. 37.

[27] Mark B. Sobell and Linda Sobell, *Behavioral Treatment of Alcohol Problems* (New York: Plenum Press, 1978), p. 74.

[28] Vaillant, p. 24.

[29] Heather and Robertson (1997), p. 98.

[30] Heather and Robertson (1997), p. 98.

[31] Stanton Peele, *Diseasing of America* (San Francisco: Jossey-Bass, 1995), p. 6.

Chapter 5

[1] Stanton Peele and Archie Brodsky, *The Truth About Addiction and Recovery* (New York: Fireside, 1992), p. 42.

[2] Stanton Peele, *Diseasing of America* (San Francisco: Jossey-Bass, 1995), p. 21.

[3] George E. Vaillant, *The Natural History of Alcoholism Revisited* (Cambridge: Harvard University Press, 1995), p. 222.

[4] S.H. Lovibond and G. Caddy, "Discriminated Aversive Control in the Moderation of Alcoholics' Drinking Behavior," *Behavior Therapy*, v. 1 (1970), pp. 437-444.

[5] Herbert Fingarette, *Heavy Drinking* (Berkeley: University of California Press; 1988), p. 124, citing G.A. Marlatt, "The Controlled Drinking Controversy," *American Psychologist*, v. 38 (1983), pp. 1097-1110.

[6] Mark B. Sobell and Linda Sobell, *Behavioral Treatment of Alcohol Problems* (New York: Plenum Press, 1978), p. 110.

[7] Sobell and Sobell, p. 155.

[8] Sobell and Sobell, p. 166.

[9] M.C. Pendery, I.M. Maltzman, and L.J. West, "Controlled Drinking by Alcoholics?: New Findings and a Reevaluation of a Major Affirmative Study," *Science*, v. 217 (1982), pp. 169-175.

[10] B.M. Dickens, A.N. Doob, O.H. Warwick, and W.C. Winegard, "Report of the Committee of Inquiry into Allegations Concernings Drs. Linda and Mark Sobell," Addiction Research Foundation (1982).

[11] R.L. Trachtenberg, "Report of the Steering Group to the Administrator, Alcohol, Drug Abuse, and Mental Heath Administration, Regarding Its Attempts to Investigate Allegations of Scientific Misconduct Concerning Drs. Mark and Linda Sobell," Alcohol, Drug Abuse, and Mental Health Administration, 1984.

[12] M. Sanchez-Craig, H. Annis, A. Bornet, and K. McDonald, "Random Assignment to Abstinence and Controlled Drinking: Evaluation of a Cognitive-Behavioral Program for Problem Drinkers," *Journal of Consulting and Clinical Psychology*, v. 52 (1984), pp. 390-403.

[13] D.W. Foy, R.G. Rychtarik, T.P. O'Brien, and L.B. Nunn, "Goal Choice of Alcoholics: Effects of Training Controlled Drinking Skills," *Journal of Clinical Psychology*, v. 34(3) (1979), pp. 781-783; R. G. Rychtarik, D.W. Foy, T. Scott, L. Lokey, and D.M. Prue, "Five to Six Year Follow-Up of Broad-Spectrum Behavioral Treatment for Alcoholism: Effects of Training Controlled Drinking Skills," *Journal of Consulting and Clinical Psychology*, v. 55 (1987), pp. 106-108.

[14] Foy et. al. (1979).

[15] W.R. Miller, "Increasing Motivation for Change," in *Handbook of Alcoholism Treatment Approaches, 2nd ed.*, Reid K. Hester and William R. Miller (eds.) (Needham Heights, MA: Allyn & Bacon, 1995), citing W.R. Miller, A.L. Leckman, H.D. Delaney, and M. Tinkcom, "Long-Term Follow-up of Behavioral Self-Control Training," *Journal of Studies on Alcohol*, v. 53 (1992), pp. 249-261.

[16] M.E. Larimer, G.A. Marlatt, J.S. Baer, L.A. Quigley, A.W. Blume, and E.H. Hawkins, "Harm Reduction for Alcohol Problems," in G. Alan Marlatt (ed.), *Harm Reduction* (New York: The Guilford Press, 1998), p. 81, citing L.C. Sobell, J.A. Cunningham, M.B. Sobell, S. Agrawal, D.R. Gavin, G.I. Leo, K.N. Singh, "Fostering Self-Change Among Problem Drinkers: A Proactive Community Intervention," *Addictive Behavior*, v. 21 (1996), pp. 817-833.

[17] M.E. Larimer, G.A. Marlatt, J.S. Baer, L.A. Quigley, A.W. Blume, and E.H. Hawkins, "Harm Reduction for Alcohol Problems," in Marlatt, p. 81.

[18] Nick Heather and Ian Robertson, *Problem Drinking, 2nd ed.* (Oxford University Press, 1989), p.158.

[19] M.E. Larimer, G.A. Marlatt, J.S. Baer, L.A. Quigley, A.W. Blume, and E.H. Hawkins, "Harm Reduction for Alcohol Problems," in Marlatt, p. 79.

[20] R.K. Hester, "Behavioral Self-Control Training," in *Handbook of Alcoholism Treatment Approaches, 2nd ed.*, Reid K. Hester and William R. Miller (eds.) (Needham Heights, MA: Allyn & Bacon, 1995), p. 149.

[21] Scott D. Miller and Insoo Kim Berg, *The Miracle Method* (New York: W.W. Norton & Company, 1995), p. 26.

[22] S. Peele, "Recovering from an All-or-Nothing Approach to Alcohol," *Psychology Today*, September/October 1996, pp. 35-43.

[23] Sobell and Sobell, p. 179.

[24] Peele, p. 198.

[25] George E. Vaillant, *The Natural History of Alcoholism Revisited* (Cambridge: Harvard University Press, 1995), p. 9.

[26] Nick Heather and Ian Robertson, *Problem Drinking, 3rd ed.* (Oxford University Press, 1997), p. 37.

[27] Heather and Robertson (1997), pp. 74-75.

[28] See also R. Room, "Alcoholism and Alcoholics Anonymous in U.S. films, 1945-1962: The Party Ends for the 'Wet Generations,'" *Journal of Studies on Alcohol*, 50(4) (1989), pp. 368-383.

Chapter 6

[1] Stanton Peele, *Diseasing of America* (San Francisco: Jossey-Bass, 1995), p. 99.

[2] Stanton Peele and Archie Brodsky, *The Truth About Addiction and Recovery* (New York: Fireside, 1992), p. 36.

[3] Peele and Brodsky (1992), pp. 30-31.

[4] Peele and Brodsky (1992), p. 37.

[5] Nick Heather and Ian Robertson, *Problem Drinking,* 2nd ed. (Oxford University Press, 1989), p. 169.

[6] Heather and Robertson, p. 60.

[7] Jack Trimpey, *The Small Book,* revised ed. (New York: Dell Publishing, 1992), p. 43.

[8] Herbert Fingarette, *Heavy Drinking* (Berkeley: The University of California Press, 1988), p. 74.

[9] Douglas Cameron, *Liberating Solutions to Alcohol Problems* (New Jersey: Jason Aronson, Inc., 1995), p. 237.

[10] George E. Vaillant, *The Natural History of Alcoholism Revisited* (Cambridge: Harvard University Press, 1995), pp. 4-5.

[11] Vaillant, p. 22.

[12] Vaillant, p. 354.

[13] David B. Morris, *Illness and Culture in the Postmodern Age* (Berkeley: University of California Press, 1998), p. 13.

[14] Vaillant, p. 44.

[15] Vaillant, p. 119.

[16] Mark B. Sobell and Linda Sobell, *Behavioral Treatment of Alcohol Problems* (New York: Plenum Press, 1978), p. 13.

[17] Fingarette, p. 26.

[18] Peele, p. 143.

[19] Peele, p. 28.

[20] 392 U.S. 514.

Chapter 7

¹ Nick Heather and Ian Robertson, *Problem Drinking, 2nd ed.* (Oxford University Press, 1989), p. 274.

² Heather and Robertson (1989), p. 283.

³ National Institute on Alcohol Abuse and Alcoholism, *Special Report on Alcohol and Health, Tenth Edition* (NIAAA, 1999), citing H.M. Annis, "Is Inpatient Rehabilitation of the Alcoholic Cost-Effective? Con Position," in *Controversies in Alcoholism and Substance Abuse*, B. Stimmel (ed.), (New York: Haworth Press, Inc. 1986), pp. 175-190.

⁴ Reid K. Hester and William R. Miller (eds.), *Handbook of Alcoholism Treatment Approaches, 2nd ed.* (Needham Heights, MA: Allyn & Bacon, 1995).

⁵ W.R. Miller, J.M. Brown, T.L. Simpson, N.S. Handmaker, T.H. Bien, L.F. Luckie, H.A. Montgomery, R.K. Hester, and J.S. Tonigan, "What Works? A Methodological Analysis of the Alcohol Treatment Outcome Literature," in Hester and Miller, p. 33.

⁶ N.L. Cooney, A. Zweben, and M.F. Fleming, "Screening for Alcohol Problems and At-Risk Drinking in Health-Care Settings," in Hester and Miller, p. 46.

⁷ Id., p. 55.

⁸ Id.

⁹ W.R. Miller, "Increasing Motivation for Change," in Hester and Miller, p. 91.

¹⁰ Id., citing J.O. Prochaska and C.C. DiClemente, "Transtheoretical Therapy: Toward a More Integrative Model of Change," *Psychotherapy: Theory, Research, and Practice*, v. 19 (1982), pp. 276-288.

¹¹ Id., p. 93.

¹² Id., pp. 93-94.

[13] Scott D. Miller and Insoo Kim Berg, *The Miracle Method* (New York: W.W. Norton & Company, 1995), p. 35-36, citing W.R. Miller, "Motivation and Treatment Goals," Drugs and Society, v. 1 (1987), pp. 133-151.

[14] W.R. Miller, "Increasing Motivation for Change," in Hester and Miller, p. 95.

[15] Id., p. 100.

[16] Id., p. 100, citing C. G. Watson, L. Jacobs, J. Pucel, C. Tilleskjor, and E.A. Hoodecheck-Schow, "The Relationship of Beliefs about Controlled Drinking to Recidivism in Alcoholic Men," *Journal of Studies on Alcohol*, v. 45 (1984), pp. 172-175.

[17] NIAAA.

[18] Id.

[19] N. Heather, "Brief Intervention Strategies," in Hester and Miller, p. 106.

[20] Id., p. 108.

[21] Id., p. 109.

[22] R.K. Hester, "Behavioral Self-Control Training," in Hester and Miller, p. 148.

[23] Id., p. 149.

[24] Id., p. 150.

[25] Id., p. 151.

[26] Id., p. 151.

[27] Id., p. 152.

[28] Id., p. 153.

[29] Id., p. 154.

[30] P. M. Monti, D.J. Rohsenow, S.M. Colby, and D.B. Abrams, "Coping and Social Skills Training," in Hester and Miller, p. 222.

[31] Id., p. 235.

[32] Heather and Robertson, p. 57.

[33] B.S. McCrady and S. I. Delaney, "Self-Help Groups," in Hester and Miller, p. 173.

[34] Nick Heather and Ian Robertson, *Problem Drinking, 3rd ed.* (Oxford University Press, 1997), p. 43.

[35] Jack Trimpey, *The Small Book, rev. ed.* (New York: Dell Publishing, 1992), p. 36.

[36] Miller and Berg, p. 84.

[37] G.A. Marlatt, "Relapse Prevention," in Hester and Miller, p. 176.

[38] Id., p. 177.

[39] Id.

[40] Id., p. 178.

[41] Id., p. 180.

[42] G.A. Marlatt, "Highlights of Harm Reduction," in G. Alan Marlatt (ed.), *Harm Reduction* (New York: The Guilford Press, 1998), p. 3.

[43] G.A. Marlatt, "Harm Reduction Around the World," in Marlatt, p. 30.

[44] G.A. Marlatt, "Basic Principles and Strategies of Harm Reduction," in Marlatt (1998), pp. 54-56.

[45] M.E. Larimer, G.A. Marlatt, J.S. Baer, L.A. Quigley, A.W. Blume, and E.H. Hawkins, "Harm Reduction for Alcohol Problems," in Marlatt (1998), p. 91.

[46] J.E. Smith and R.J. Meyers, "The Community Reinforcement Approach," in Hester and Miller, p. 251.

[47] Id., p. 264.

[48] Id., p. 253.

[49] Id., p. 257.

[50] Stanton Peele, *Diseasing of America* (San Francisco: Jossey-Bass, 1995), p. 262.

[51] Peele, p. 257.

[52] R.K. Fuller, "Antidipsotropic Medications," in Hester and Miller, p. 127.

[53] Id., p. 124.

[54] B.A. Johnson, J.D. Roache, M.A. Javors, C.C. DiClemente, C.R. Cloninger, T.J. Prihoda, P.S. Bordnick, N. Ait-Daoud, J. Hensler, "Ondansatron for Reduction of Drinking Among Biologically Predisposed Alcoholic Patients: A Randomized Controlled Trial," *Journal of the American Medical Association*, August 23, 2000, pp. 963-979.

[55] NIAAA; see also J.C. Garbutt, S.L. West, T.S. Carey, K.N. Lohr, F.T. Crews, "Pharmacological Treatment of Alcohol Dependence: A Review of the Evidence," *Journal of the American Medical Association*, April 14, 1999, pp. 1318-1325.

[56] NIAAA, citing S.S. O'Malley, A.J. Jaffe, G. Chang, R.S. Schottenfeld, R.E. Meyer, and B. Rounsaville, "Naltrexone and Coping Skills Therapy for Alcohol Dependence: A Controlled Study," Achives of General Psychiatry, 49 (11) (1992), pp. 881-887.

[57] J.P. Allen and R.M. Kadden, "Matching Clients to Alcohol Treatments," in Hester and Miller, p. 279.

[58] Id., p. 284.

[59] NIAAA.

[60] W.R. Miller and R.K. Hester, "Treatment for Alcohol Problems: Toward an Informed Eclecticism," in Hester and Miller, p. 9.

●

Permissions

•

Index